The
ESSENTIAL
GUIDE *to*
DELIVERANCE

Books by Larry Richards*

735 Baffling Bible Questions Answered

Becoming One in the Spirit

The Believer's Guidebook

The Believer's Praise Book

The Bible Answer Handbook

A Child's Life of Christ

A Guy and a Girl

Bible Difficulties Solved

Born to Grow

Enriching Your Marriage

The Essential Guide to Deliverance

Everyday Bible Insights

The Full Armor of God

How the Church Can Help the Family Face the Future

The International Bible Field Guide

It Couldn't Just Happen

Living in Touch with God

Love Your Neighbor

Men of the Bible

One Way

Our Life Together

Promises for the Graduate

Remarriage: A Healing Gift from God

Reshaping Evangelical Higher Education

Revolutionize Your Bible Study

Satan Exposed

Spiritual Warfare Jesus' Way

The Screwloose Lectures

Talkable Bible Stories

Teachers: Teaching with Love

Three Churches in Renewal

Tomorrow's Church Today

Understanding God's Promises

What's in the Bible for Teens?

When It Hurts Too Much to Wait

When Life Is Unfair

When People You Trust Let You Down

Wisdom for the Graduate

*This is a partial listing

The

ESSENTIAL
GUIDE *to*
DELIVERANCE

Finding True Freedom *in* Christ

LARRY RICHARDS

Chosen
a division of Baker Publishing Group
Minneapolis, Minnesota

© 2016 by Lawrence O. Richards

Published by Chosen Books
11400 Hampshire Avenue South
Bloomington, Minnesota 55438
www.chosenbooks.com

Chosen Books is a division of
Baker Publishing Group, Grand Rapids, Michigan

Printed in the United States of America

Library of Congress Control Number: 2016938478

ISBN 978-0-8007-9587-0

Cover design by Gearbox

16 17 18 19 20 21 22   7 6 5 4 3 2 1

Contents

Part 1

UNDERSTANDING *the* PROBLEM

1

Demons at the Dinner Table

We had just finished Sunday dinner when the subject of demons came up.

The two couples with us attend a Sunday school class my wife and I teach. Dave and Sharon and Steve and Linette are all in their late fifties, pushing sixty. They have been regular churchgoers and are serious about their faith. But as we talked it was clear they knew almost nothing about demons.

That is not surprising. The churches they had attended, like most churches today, had never taught about demons or the influence they seek to have in Christians' lives. Our friends trust the Bible, and they know that Jesus confronted demons and evil spirits. But they were totally in the dark about what demons do today. They did not trust Hollywood's portrayals of demons. Somehow the gruesome scenes of supposed demonic possession in such movies as *The Exorcist* did not ring true. And they wondered: What do demons do? Can Christians be "possessed"? How do demons gain a foothold in a person's life? Do you have to be a priest or minister or have special training to get rid of demons? What is involved in getting a demon out of someone's life?

For the next hour or two I answered their questions and tried to give them a clear and simple picture of demonization and spiritual warfare. I know that many, if not most, Christians here in the West are as unaware of demonic influence and activity as our friends. And I can understand why.

After four years in the Navy and completing my B.A. at the University of Michigan, I went to what I considered the finest seminary available: Dallas Theological Seminary in Dallas, Texas.

Unlike many seminaries, Dallas had a rigorous four-year program leading to a master's in theology. Each semester we had to carry eighteen to twenty hours of classes, including Greek and Hebrew. In those four years we studied every book of the Bible, as well as attended classes on preaching, Christian education, theology, hermeneutics and all the other subjects the seminary considered necessary to equip graduates thoroughly for ministry. But we did not have even one class that dealt with spiritual warfare or the nature of demonic activity in today's world. We had a text that covered what the Bible says about demons and evil spirits. But we had no training in recognizing demonic activity or in ministering to those who were under demonic attack.

My seminary experience was not unusual. Training in this area is not common in our seminaries, although there are one or two notable exceptions. As a result, most pastors today are inexperienced in spiritual warfare. It is hardly surprising that our friends had never heard sermons or been offered classes in demonization and deliverance.

Adding to the problem, too many in ministry are afraid to look deeply into this area. In another dinner table experience, this time in California, several pastors were talking about their ministries. One of them confessed that he was dealing with deep depression that he could not throw off, even though God was blessing his ministry. As he continued to share, a longtime friend of mine who has a deliverance ministry noted that what was happening to the pastor had all the earmarks of demonic oppression. The pastor was horrified. So my friend asked, if you were under attack by demons, wouldn't you want to know? So you could be delivered? The frightened pastor shook his head. No! He would rather go on suffering than even consider the possibility of demonic influence.

I can understand how he felt. When I graduated from seminary, getting involved with demons was one of two things I determined never to do. Later I visited a classmate who had a church in Seattle and was dealing with the demonic regularly. He shared his stories with me, but I still wanted nothing to do with demons or deliverance. I continued to feel this way for many years. After all, I had been called to teach Christian education and Bible in Wheaton College Graduate School. I had published several influential textbooks. I was in demand as a speaker and often taught courses in my field at places like Princeton Theological Seminary and Talbot Seminary.

Then some ten years ago, I was led to start a series of fiction books tracing the war between angels and demons from Creation to history's end. While the books are fiction, they are deeply rooted in Scripture. But as I wrote the novels, it was clear that both I and my family were under some sort of spiritual attack. Apparently Satan did not approve of my subject matter. At that point it was clear I needed to learn more about demonization—how to recognize it and how to deal with it.

I renewed my focus on exploring the Bible, and found that the subject of demonic activity is clearly present in the Old Testament and the epistles, as well as the gospels. It appears more evident in the gospels, where terms like *demon* and *evil spirit* are commonly used. But I realized that the epistles adopt the vocabulary of Greek culture and refer to spirit beings with words like *powers, rulers* and *authorities.* There was far more in Scripture about demonic activity than I had realized, despite my intense seminary education!

Along with studying Scripture I began to read books on spiritual warfare. To be honest, some of them seemed to take the Hollywood approach and feature only the most unusual manifestations. But other books shared principles and practices that reflected an everyday rather than sensationalized approach to deliverance from demonic influence. I talked with reliable people who had deliverance ministries. As I learned more and more, I began to share what I was learning through the blog www.demondope.com.

The turning point came when I was invited to teach a course on the spirit world at a seminary in California. The one-week course culminated in what I call a Freedom Workshop that is open to the public. My students were there, ready to counsel and pray with anyone who was concerned about possible demonic influence in his or her life.

Freedom Workshops are an intensive study of Ephesians, which, I have come to realize, is a handbook on spiritual warfare that Paul developed for young first-century churches. At the end of the day-and-a-half workshop, a number of people asked for counseling and prayer. Some of them were clearly bound by demonic activity. That last afternoon truly became the first step toward freedom for some of the men and women who attended.

To continue to support those who were being delivered, several students met in small groups to study together and support each other. I sent them curriculum every week. During this time I heard from both my students and those they ministered to that people were being delivered and finding freedom from demonic oppression. If you care to look, what I teach in Freedom Workshops, including a study guide for small groups, is covered in the book *The Full Armor of God* (Chosen, 2013).

By this point I was fully convinced. Not only are demons and evil spirits real, they are active in the lives of believers and unbelievers alike. I was also convinced that Jesus can and will deliver those who are under the influence of demons. Victims truly can experience freedom from oppression!

Since that first Freedom Workshop I have taught many more. I have experienced the privilege of casting demons from hurting people and seeing them step into freedom. I do not have a "deliverance ministry." In most ways I am like the four friends gathered with us for that Sunday dinner. But now when God brings people who are oppressed into my life, I know how to recognize and deal with the demons involved.

That is why Chosen asked me to write this book. It is a book for the average Christian, who knows little or nothing about demons and deliverance. It is exciting for me to be able to share with you what I have learned and experienced. It is exciting because I know with certainty that you will at some point have to deal with demonic influence on yourself or come into contact with the demonized. People who have written to me, and many whom I have spoken with, tell of their fears for family members and friends or themselves. They want to know, "Can it be demons?"

In this book I will take you through the basics. You will discover how demons can impact our lives. You will learn how to recognize demonic presence. You will learn how to identify specific demons. And the most amazing thing you will learn is that, in the name and power of Jesus, you, too, can expel evil spirits. You, too, can give the gift of freedom to the oppressed.

TO TALK ABOUT

It would be helpful for you as we go along to write down your answers to the questions that conclude each chapter. Making lists will focus your study and highlight the specific information you seek.

1. What things do you *know* about demons and evil spirits?
2. What impressions about demons and evil spirits do you have that you are not quite sure of?
3. What are three questions you hope this book will answer?

2

Demons on Screen

It was late Saturday afternoon. I had just finished conducting my Freedom Workshop at Seattle's First Presbyterian Church, and a number of people were standing around, talking. A friend and longtime pastor, Gib Martin, was speaking to a rather strange looking young man.

Gib is the friend I mentioned in the first chapter who has been on the front lines in dealing with the demonic, both in his church and in a recovery center his church supported. Of all the people I know, Gib has had the most hands-on experience in dealing with demons and in delivering victims of demonic oppression.

I walked over to Gib and the young man, David, who was dressed in aged working clothes and who seemed somewhat disconnected during our conversation. As we talked, David told us about his life. He had been brought up in a gypsy family. All of his female relatives were deeply involved in the occult, making their living by fortune-telling, palm reading and interpreting tarot cards. For them, cursing others, breaking curses, creating love potions and performing other occult services was a way of life. From childhood David had felt an overwhelming sense of darkness and lack of control. He had no home and was currently living in his car. He had stopped at the church looking for a meal and said that he had no idea how he happened to end up in my Freedom Workshop. But as the workshop ended, David wanted desperately to talk to someone and to get help.

I learned later that as Gib, David and I sat down together to talk, my wife, who was on the other side of the church, felt an overwhelming sense of evil. She sat down and began to pray desperately for Gib and me. Something was there, something very real, something truly evil and threatening.

As we listened to David's story, both Gib and I were convinced that David was demonized. That word *demonized*, typically translated "demon-possessed" in the gospels, does not really mean "possessed," as if the victim were taken over and totally controlled by one or more demons. *Demonized* does mean that, in some way, demons have established a foothold in a victim's life and to a certain extent exert influence over him or her. As David told his story, we had no doubt that evil spirits, another term the New Testament uses to identify demons, were actively and powerfully at work in his life.

Gib and I both sensed that this was not the moment to try to cast out the demon or demons who were oppressing David. We told David we would pray for him, and we urged him to come to church the next day and attend Gib's Sunday school class. As we began to pray, I reached out to "lay hands" on David, the biblical practice of gently placing one's hands on a person being prayed for, when Gib grabbed my arm quickly and shook his head. We continued to pray for David, and when the prayer time ended David promised to return the next day.

Later I asked Gib why he had stopped me from laying hands on David as we prayed. "I sensed that the demons oppressing David are pretty powerful," Gib explained, and told me of a time when he had laid hands on a person in the grip of powerful evil spirits. As he placed his hands on the individual to pray for him, Gib felt a shock as if struck in the chest by a powerful blow. Gib cast out the demon, but for several days he was laid up in bed, almost unable to move. Three of the elders of his church came and prayed for him, and he recovered quickly. But each of the three elders experienced disabling effects for several days.

You can imagine how grateful I was to have a wise mentor and friend at that Freedom Workshop!

On Sunday David showed up and went to Gib's class. He had had to fight overwhelming impulses to stay away that grew stronger as he approached the church. But David was desperate to change his life and find freedom rather than keep on living in bondage. Now, with the prayer support of Gib's class, it was time to deal with the demons who had oppressed David for most of his life. Claiming authority over the demons in the name of Jesus, and as the class members added their prayers, Gib forced the evil spirits present to identify themselves. One by one Gib ordered them to leave David and never return. In all, thirteen evil spirits were identified and cast out of David that morning.

Of course, the story does not end here. David had experienced the power of Jesus to deliver him. For the first time in his memory the sense of oppression left him. David accepted Christ, and the last I heard he was being discipled by a friend of Gib and growing in his faith.

On the Big Screen

America's fascination with the supernatural is reflected in the proliferation of movies featuring demons and the occult. A quick search on the Internet provided me with a list of some 41 movies, headlined of course by that standard, *The Exorcist*.

In *The Exorcist* a Catholic priest confronts a demon who has taken possession of a young girl named Regan. The scenes are laced with sexual perversion, cursing, exhibitions of superhuman strength, levitation, unrestrainable violence and speaking in tongues, and the face of the supposed demon is shown. As a noxious liquid spews from Regan's mouth, the demon is finally expelled. (By the way, the liquid spewing from the girl's mouth was Anderson's pea soup. Campbell's did not produce an appropriate effect.)

The film, which claims to be "loosely based on real-life events," has earned more money than any other horror film, although the film writer insists that it is not a horror show at all but a "supernatural detective story." At any rate, *The Exorcist* has spawned four additional films, two sequels and two prequels.

It is not surprising that the popularity of *The Exorcist* moved Hollywood to make a number of demon movies. At least ten of them are supposedly based on "terrifying real-life cases of demonic possession." Among them are:

The Entity, portraying a single mom with four children in Culver City, California, who claims she is being raped by invisible attackers;

Deliver Us from Evil, where unseen forces control the lives, emotions and thoughts of a family that moves into a house where another family was murdered the year before;

The Exorcism of Emily Rose, the story of Anneliese Michel, who was convinced she was possessed, screamed helplessly for hours and attacked others aggressively. She died of malnutrition and dehydration;

The Haunting of Connecticut, featuring demons who wander the halls of a home that the family discovers was once a funeral home. An exorcism was performed on the house, but the family was driven out;

The Possession, the story of a girl who is under the control of an evil spirit living in a wine cabinet that once belonged to a Holocaust survivor;

The Changeling, in which unexplained events in a rented house lead a writer, played by George C. Scott, to seek the help of a medium;

The Amityville Horror, once again, a house, where grisly murders took place thirteen months before, is the scene of the demonic possession of George Lutz, head of the family. After 28 days of terror and unexplained phenomena, the family moves out;

The Devils, a seventeenth-century priest is accused of using sorcery against nuns in a convent, who curse and scream and claim they are possessed. The priest is burned at the stake.

And, of course, a multitude of movies make no claim to real-life origins. These include *Hellraiser, Demons, The Devil's Rock, Demon Knight, Night of the Demons, Insidious, Pumpkinhead 1* and *2, The Ninth Gate*. Movies featuring demons are obviously popular and profitable. And they have much in common. They feature supernatural manifestations, such as objects moving without apparent cause and strange sounds in the night. Most significantly they contain images of individuals who are supposedly demon-possessed, who are out of control and who manifest terrifying behaviors. Now and then, as in *The Exorcist*, we are given a glimpse of the demons themselves, all ugly and frightening.

It is hardly surprising, considering the pervasiveness of Hollywood's portrayal of the demonic, that there is so little awareness of real demons and so little understanding of how they impact the lives of ordinary Christians.

On the Tube

Films like the ones above appeal generally to 18- to 34-year-olds. Most older folk do not generally spend money on horror movies. At the same time, we can hardly escape the 36 shows currently on TV that feature the demonic; shows like *Angel, Dark Tales, Lucifer, All Souls* and *The X-Files*. And we are all too likely to pause to watch one of the 118 paranormal shows that can be found on such major channels and networks as ABC, TBS, A&E, CBS, UPN, Syfy, Fox, History, Discovery and even MTV. Filmed with filters providing an eerie green tint and backed by equally eerie music and sound effects, such shows fascinate those who watch them, despite the failure of investigative teams' efforts to produce ghosts or demons on camera.

The proliferation of such programs makes it clear that many viewers are fascinated by the supernatural—and build their impressions of ghosts, angels and demons on what they see on the big screen and on television.

Deliverance Ministry Rallies

If we define *deliverance ministry* as "the casting out of evil spirits believed to cause some affliction," its appearance in the United States emerged from the impact of *The Exorcist* on our culture.

Exorcism, of course, was common historically in the experience of the early Church; only later was it captured as a ritual that could be performed solely by a Roman Catholic priest. The idea of holding rallies where crowds can witness for themselves groups of the afflicted being set free from demons is a modern invention. Often in these rallies individuals who seem to be oppressed by demons appear to lose control as they shout, weep, curse and even fall to the floor wriggling like snakes. A number of such deliverance gatherings are available for viewing on YouTube.

From the public's perspective, based on movies, television and some portrayals of deliverance ministry, the "demons" act in overt and frightening ways. In all this, the image of demonization that has filtered into our culture is hardly a biblical one. The media depiction, certainly, is designed to sensationalize the demonic and to provide the audience with the titillation of vicarious fear. It is not a surprise, then, that Christians who have never been taught about demons and demonization develop many ideas about the supernatural that are, simply, wrong. In this book, you and I will be examining the biblical text and build our understanding of demonization from Scripture.

Good Demons?

While most media presentations about demons are designed to stimulate fear and horror, a contrasting view of dark spiritual entities is also growing rapidly in our society. This is the view promoted by Wicca, also termed Pagan Witchcraft, and the some-150 other neopagan faiths that have taken root in the West in the past century.

Dedicated to what they call "white" witchcraft, modern witches believe in a spiritual universe existing alongside our material universe. Christians also believe in a spiritual world but view its occupants and their intentions quite differently. Witches contend that the spiritual realm is populated by gods, goddesses, the spirits of the dead, angels and demons, all of whom are beneficial, eager to help the living in any way possible.

Those who practice Wicca seek the help of these various spirit beings for their clients' needs, including contacting loved ones who have died. Along with providing palm and tarot readings, they urge clients and friends to open themselves to the spirit world and invite a "spirit guide" into their lives.

According to the Witch's Voice blog, there are currently 109 pagan schools that offer courses on witchcraft and the occult. One of them, the Witch School located in Salem, Massachusetts, boasts several thousand correspondence school students who are studying to be ordained as witches. Another, New York City's Academy of Pagan Studies, offers a degree path to priest or priestess, which enables a person to be ordained as "Reverend" in New York State.

While the Bible prohibits all such traffic with the spirit world (see Deuteronomy 18:9–13), the notion that contact with spirits is something to be desired permeates the neopagan subculture and is spreading through the dominant culture.

Back to David

In this chapter I have decried the way demons and demonization have been portrayed on the big screen, on the tube and even in many contemporary deliverance crusades. The vivid, frightening and obviously supernatural manifestations that they feature promote a distinctly non-biblical view of demonization. I have also taken a brief look at the growing neopagan view of the spirit world, with its emphasis on making contact with spirits, which the Bible prohibits in no uncertain terms, as any spirits responding can be nothing other than demons.

So you might be wondering why I began this chapter by relating my experience with David. You might ask: "Isn't David's story—and especially Gib's experience of laying hands on a person in the grip of a very powerful demon—just as 'sensational' as what movies and TV attempt to portray?"

Actually, no. True, Gib's experience could be enhanced to show him flying across the room after touching the demonized individual. But that is not what happened. And even more to the point, in some forty years of casting out evil spirits and releasing victims from the influence of demons, what Gib described happened only one time.

But let's go back to the first time we met David after my Freedom Workshop in that Presbyterian church. Imagine a film crew sets up the camera, adjusts the lights, and the director calls out, "Action." Yet all they have to film is three men standing around talking, then sitting down to talk more. One of them is wearing a suit (Gib), another shirt and tie (me), and the third rough working clothes and heavy workman's boots. As we talk the face of the one called David shows his anxiety and unhappiness. The faces of the two men talking with David show concern as they listen intently. But there is no shouting, no uncontrolled waving of arms, no falling on the floor and wriggling like snakes. In fact, there are absolutely no manifestations of the demons who oppress David that the camera can capture!

Oh, the camera might shift to show my wife, seated on the other side of the church, her head bowed in prayer. But this is nothing like the graphic and impactful images featured in movies, on TV or even in video reports of mass deliverance meetings.

Everything seems so terribly *ordinary*.

Even if the director does not give up and sends the crew to Gib's Sunday school class the next day, there will be nothing exciting to film. They will catch the young man coming into the room to be greeted by Gib. They will hear Gib talking with him as the whole class joins in prayer. They will hear the two men talk about David's family and relatives, and how long he has been troubled. They could film as Gib identifies and then speaks calmly to the demons infecting David, ordering them out. And they could film the expression on David's face as he senses each of the thirteen demons withdrawing from his life. As the demons leave there will be little or nothing to film, although at times when a demon leaves he might give his victim a final shake.

They could film the class joining Gib and Dave in praise for the deliverance. And then they would have nothing to watch but Gib as he goes back to teaching the lesson he has prepared.

It all really does seem so terribly ordinary.

Deeply disappointed, the director and his film crew take down their equipment and leave. "What a pity," one says, "that there weren't any *real* demons there."

Rethinking the "Ordinary"

That, of course, is the point of this chapter. There are real demons. Real demons were there, and they were cast out. Demons really do take up residence in the lives of Christians and non-Christians, and they do all they can to torment and make life unproductive. Typically a victim is not even aware that he or she is demonized, although the inward and personal effects of demonization are likely to grow more and more obvious to others and to the demonized themselves as time goes by. But even then, most are unlikely to identify demonization as the issue. We have been programmed by the media to associate demonization with the unexplained bump in the night, the glimpse of a "ghost" in a hallway, the uncontrollable outburst or the sudden chill that comes over us when we sense something eerie is about.

Honestly, if you check back on your lists of what you know about demons and demonization, I think you might be surprised or chagrined to find that your ideas have been shaped to some extent by the media. We have hardly been taught to view demonization or casting out evil spirits as something ordinary.

As we go on in this book, however, we will discover that demonization and casting out evil spirits are far more ordinary than we have suspected. And we will find that dealing with evil spirits is one of the ways to victorious Christian living.

TO TALK ABOUT

1. What movies or TV shows about demons or the supernatural have you seen? What dominant impression did they leave you with?

2. Go back over your lists of things you said you know or think you know about demons and demonization. Can you trace where these beliefs came from?

3. What is your reaction to the author's assertion that demons and demonization are essentially "ordinary"?

3

Diagnosing Demonization

As we read the gospels we get the impression that demonization is rampant. Again and again we read things like: "When evening came, they brought to Him many who were demon-possessed [literally, *demonized*, a word we will use from now on where the English translation has *demon-possessed*]; and He cast out the spirits with a word, and healed all who were ill" (Matthew 8:16 NASB). The other gospels support Matthew's testimony. Mark writes of a time when the people of one town "brought to Jesus all the sick and [demonized]" and tells us that Jesus not only healed the sick but "drove out many demons" (see Mark 1:32, 34). Luke tells us that crowds gathered from all over Judea and Jerusalem to seek Jesus' help and that "those troubled by evil spirits were cured" (Luke 6:18). In fact, the days Jesus was on earth, and particularly during His public ministry, seem marked by an unusual amount of demonic activity in the Holy Land.

We should not be surprised at this. The prophet Daniel predicted that from the date a Persian ruler issued a decree to rebuild

Jerusalem, the Savior promised in the Old Testament would appear. This was not hidden from Satan, recorded as it is in the sacred writings (cf. 1 Peter 1:10–12). The predicted time would clearly mark a clash of kingdoms, the kingdom of evil and the Kingdom of God. It is not surprising that Satan's minions should be especially active at this pivotal moment in history.

Even if demons were particularly active in the days Christ lived and taught on earth, their effect on human beings provides us with clues for diagnosing demonization today. And it also warns us against going overboard in a search for a demonic cause of all our troubles.

Demons in the Ancient World

The contrast between the view toward demons in the ancient world and references to demons in the Old Testament is fascinating. While the Old Testament portrays demons as energizing the pagan gods that the people surrounding Israel worshiped, there is no particular emphasis on demons or demonic activity within the community of Israel. Languages of the surrounding peoples, such as the Samarians, Assyrians and Babylonians, are filled with hundreds of words for various evil spirits, demons and deities. While the rulers of pagan nations valued messages from these deities as a source of guidance, ordinary people viewed them as deeply hostile to human beings. Much of the literature of the time is devoted to devising spells that would help persons avoid or reverse the harmful effects of demons.

Jewish literature from just before and around the time of Christ shows a fascination with demons, as in *Testament of Solomon*, which purports to relate King Solomon's interviews with demons. Even in the wider Roman world Jewish exorcists were viewed with special respect, for they were supposed to know the secret name of their powerful unseen God, which they could use in the incantations Jew and pagan alike relied on to dominate and control demons. As we read the gospels, we meet a population that was not surprised by the presence of so many demonized but was shocked at Jesus' ability to cast out demons "with a word" (Matthew 8:16). It was the complete and utter domination of demons by Jesus without the use of incantations or ritualized spells that stunned the crowds.

This, of course, does not help particularly in our quest to diagnose demonization today. For that let's begin by meeting several of the demonized individuals who were delivered by Jesus and whose stories are told in the gospels.

Meet the Demonized

The churchgoer. His story is told in both Mark 1:23–27 and Luke 4:33–36.

> In the synagogue there was a man possessed by a demon, an evil spirit. He cried out at the top of his voice, "Ha! What do you want with us, Jesus of Nazareth? Have you come to destroy us? I know who you are—the Holy One of God!"
>
> Luke 4:33–34

The story of the churchgoer is significant. Apparently he had gathered with his neighbors and friends to worship at the local synagogue. The chances are he was a hardworking Jewish man, almost indistinguishable from others in his community. We do not know what symptoms of demonization he might have been exhibiting, but they were not so extreme that his friends were moved to bring him to Jesus for healing. He seemed to fit in with his neighbors, coming with them to the synagogue. There are no signs of demonization reported, but suddenly the demon infecting him cried out when Jesus appeared.

The text of Luke tells us that after Jesus commanded the demon sternly to leave the man, the demon threw the man down without injuring him and left. In the presence of Jesus, the shocked demon revealed himself. The chances are no one in that community, including the man himself, had any suspicion that he had been demonized.

While this story does not help us diagnose demonization in individuals today, it provides an important reminder. Demons do not want to be exposed. They want to remain hidden in our lives where they can damage us without threat of being expelled.

The mute men. Two gospels tell of individuals who were mute because of demonization. One story is told in Matthew 9:32–33, given below, the other in Luke 11:14.

> While they were going out, a man who was [demonized] and could not talk was brought to Jesus. And when the demon was driven out, the man who had been mute spoke. The crowd was amazed and said, "Nothing like this has ever been seen in Israel."

The stories of the mute individuals teach us that demons do have some power to inhibit natural functions. We need to be careful not to use this as a criterion, however, because there can be causes of an inability to speak that have nothing to do with demons. A disability could possibly be a sign of demonization, but it need not be.

The crippled woman. The crippled woman's story is told in Luke 13. Here is another individual with a physical disability. Luke tells us:

On a Sabbath Jesus was teaching in one of the synagogues, and a woman was there who had been crippled by a spirit for eighteen years. She was bent over and could not straighten up at all. When Jesus saw her, he called her forward and said to her, "Woman, you are set free from your infirmity." Then he put his hands on her, and immediately she straightened up and praised God.

Luke 13:10–13

When the ruler of the synagogue objected to Jesus healing on the Sabbath, Christ responded, "Should not this woman, a daughter of Abraham, whom Satan has kept bound for eighteen long years, be set free on the Sabbath day from what bound her?" (verse 16).

Again we see the power of demons to cause physical disabilities. This story, however, adds important information. The text states specifically that this woman had been bound by Satan for eighteen years. Apparently something had happened to her eighteen years earlier that had provided an opening for the demon who had kept her bound.

Two children. Both Matthew and Mark tell of a Canaanite woman who came to Jesus with a daughter who was "suffering terribly from [demonization]" (Matthew 15:22; see Mark 7:25). We are told nothing of the daughter's symptoms, but Jesus honored the woman's request and "her daughter was healed from that very hour" (Matthew 15:28).

We are given more information in the story about a boy who is demonized. Matthew tells us:

When they came to the crowd, a man approached Jesus and knelt before him. "Lord, have mercy on my son," he said. "He has seizures and is suffering greatly. He often falls into the fire or into the water.

I brought him to your disciples, but they could not heal him." . . .
Jesus rebuked the demon, and it came out of the boy, and he was
healed from that moment.

Matthew 17:14–16, 18

In the case of the woman who was crippled for eighteen years,
we might suppose that something happened eighteen years before
that made her vulnerable to demonic oppression. In the case of the
two children we simply do not know what gave the demons access
to them or the right to trouble them so terribly. This is something
we will explore in later chapters. What we do see is that, again,
severe physical disability was the dominant symptom of demonization of these two young people. And our text tells us that Jesus
took authority over the demons, and the children were healed.

Other references. There are additional references to demonization
in the gospels and in Acts. Luke 8:2 tells us that Mary Magdalene
was possessed by seven demons. Acts 16 tells the story of a girl who
was a fortune-teller. Apparently the demons enabled her to have
some glimpse into the future. Luke describes her as a "slave girl
who had a spirit by which she predicted the future. She earned a
great deal of money for her owners by fortune-telling" (Acts 16:16).
Paul commanded the spirit in the name of Jesus to come out of the
girl, and "at that moment the spirit left her" (Acts 16:18). Certain
occult abilities can be symptoms of demonization.

Unhelpful Lists

While we glean some information from these stories, it seems that
none of the people we meet on the pages of Scripture provides

definitive information about the symptoms of demonization. Possibly for that reason, a number of individuals who are involved in deliverance ministry today have developed their own lists of symptoms. Below are some of the common denominators that deliverance ministers suggest could indicate demonization:

1. Hatred of God, the Bible and the Jewish people
2. Physical maladies that have no identifiable cause
3. Suicidal tendencies
4. Terrorizing nightmares
5. Rage, sometimes to the point of murder
6. Overwhelming depression
7. Withdrawal from loved ones
8. Suspicion of others
9. Unfounded fears
10. Feelings of invulnerability

I do not doubt that those who minister deliverance have seen all of these manifestations in those who are demonized. At the same time, there is no question that each of these symptoms can occur without any demonic involvement. Suicidal tendencies, nightmares, murderous rage and hostility are all too common in our culture.

So again we are left with uncertainty. Can we diagnose demonization? And if so, how do we diagnose demonization?

The Demoniac of Gadara

One particular story of demonization is reported in each of the three synoptic gospels. The repetition tells us that this story is especially significant. As we look at it closely, we find that it does provide important clues to symptoms of demonization. Luke gives us the following description of events that occurred when Jesus stepped out of a boat onto the land of the Gadarenes.

> When Jesus stepped ashore, he was met by a [demonized] man from the town. For a long time this man had not worn clothes or lived in a house, but had lived in the tombs. When he saw Jesus, he cried out and fell at his feet, shouting at the top of his voice, "What do you want with me, Jesus, Son of the Most High God? I beg you, don't torture me!" For Jesus had commanded the evil spirit to come out of the man. Many times it had seized him, and though he was chained hand and foot and kept under guard, he had broken his chains and had been driven by the demon into solitary places.
>
> Luke 8:27–29

Matthew adds the following information. This man, and a companion not mentioned by Mark or Luke, was "so violent that no one could pass that way" (Matthew 8:28). Mark gives us this important detail: "Night and day among the tombs and in the hills he would cry out and cut himself with stones" (Mark 5:5).

What is important for us about these descriptions is that we are given a fuller picture of demonization. The demoniac of Gadara reminds us that when attempting to diagnose demonization we need to look for a *pattern* of symptoms—a number of categories occurring together rather than a single symptom. In *Spiritual Warfare Jesus' Way* (Chosen, 2014), I provide a careful analysis of the symptoms this demoniac displayed.

There are social symptoms. In the first century a Jewish man's identity was found in his relationships. That this man left his family and his community to live "in the tombs" is significant. It is clear he was attempting to isolate himself. Today this is one of the most evident symptoms of possible demonization. Efforts by family and friends to reach out and draw the individual back into a closer relationship tend to be rejected.

There are interpersonal symptoms. This man was so hostile it was dangerous for anyone to come near him (see Matthew 8:28). Frequently those who ask me about their loved ones see frightening changes in them—particularly the increase of hostility and threats. This hostility might also be expressed as violence, as with a physically abusive spouse. Hostility and threats of violence, combined with movement toward isolation, are among the strongest indicators of possible demonization.

There are moral symptoms. In the first century the moral code emphasized modesty. The image of the demoniac without clothing, showing his failure to respect others' sensibilities, is especially noteworthy. When a person today acts in ways that show he or she is unwilling to consider the feelings and values of others, this marks an abandonment of morality and rejection of society's moral code. It is another indication of an individual's attempt to isolate him or herself from significant personal relationships.

There are mental symptoms. Luke tells us that after Jesus cast out the demons, the man was "sitting at Jesus' feet, dressed and in his right mind" (Luke 8:35). The man is now dressed, no longer rejecting the moral code of his community. He is sitting with Jesus and the disciples, no longer rejecting relationships. He is sitting quietly, no longer violent. And he is "in his right mind." The translation *right mind* comes from a compound Greek word that indicates he was thinking clearly and judging correctly. A demonized person's thought processes are likely to be corrupted. So another possible symptom of demonization is an individual's tendency to think and say things that are distorted and appear "strange."

There are physical symptoms. As we have noted, physical symptoms are particularly difficult to categorize when considering demonization because there are many natural causes of sicknesses and disabilities. In the case of the Gadarene demoniac, the amazing bursts of strength that allowed him to break chains were unusual and likely demonically driven, although this phenomenon is reported now and then by those in deliverance ministries. Again, it is best not to consider any one symptom as conclusive evidence of demonization but rather view it alongside other categories of symptoms.

There are psychological symptoms. It is Mark who pictures the demoniac crying out and cutting himself with stones (see Mark 5:5). Research today, which has explored the roots of self-mutilation, views the act as an expression of self-loathing and as evidence of crushing anxiety or despair. Shame and guilt also seem to be present. Demons may not cause such psychological symptoms, but demons can and do exaggerate emotions that are already present.

There are spiritual symptoms. An individual who is demonized generally shows ambivalence toward spiritual things. Mark tells us that the man with the evil spirit came from the tombs "to meet" Jesus. The implication in Matthew 8:28 is that his initial intention was to attack those who landed on his shore. But "when he saw Jesus from a distance, he ran and fell on his knees in front of him" (Mark 5:6). When the man recognized Jesus, he drew closer, despite the fact that the demons within him were terrified. As I noted in *Spiritual Warfare Jesus' Way*:

> Spiritual ambivalence is often present when a believer is demonized. The Christian wants to pray but evil thoughts intrude. He goes to church but cannot stay awake during the sermon. He tries

to read the Bible but cannot seem to grasp the meaning of the words. This pattern of ambivalence toward spiritual things is far more characteristic of demonization than constant, open hostility.

The story of the demoniac, with its array of symptoms in evidence, helps confirm our understanding that we cannot focus on any one factor if we hope to diagnose demonization in our own lives or in the life of a friend or family member. It is when we see a number of these categories occurring together that we have good reason to suspect demonization.

Diagnosing Demonization

Demons are real. The stories in Scripture show us the breadth of influence that they can and do have on our lives and our daily experiences. But at the same time, it is not easy to diagnose demonization. All too often a demon's activity can masquerade as behavior that we consider "natural." What could be more common than road rage, the grip of an overwhelming temptation, bitterness, isolation, moral decay, self-destruction, unforgiveness, illness, disability or feelings of guilt and shame? All these are things that human beings are heir to, making it difficult to distinguish between our human frailty and the presence of a demon gaining a foothold in our lives and exaggerating our natural failings.

As we move on in this book, we will look at how our suspicions of demonization can be confirmed. But first we need to answer some questions about demons themselves. What are they? Where did they come from? What is their mission today? And what will happen to them at history's end? These are the topics of our next chapters.

TO TALK ABOUT

1. Do you know anyone who you think might be demonized? What makes you suspicious?
2. Why does the author warn against taking any one symptom as proof of demonization?
3. What seems to you to make diagnosing demonization so difficult?

4

Will the Real Demons
Please Stand Up?

Years ago I used to watch a game show on television. Three contestants, each claiming to be the rightful bearer of a name and occupation being described by the moderator, faced a panel of celebrities. The celebrities then asked questions designed to help them identify which one of the three was telling the truth and which two were imposters. After the celebrities' choices were made, the moderator would say, "Will the real [name] please stand up?"

When dealing with demons we might feel like those panel members who have to maneuver past deception and lies to get to the truth.

Belief in evil spirits is as old as humanity. In ancient Mesopotamia expectant mothers quaked at the thought that the demon goddess Lamashtu might be stalking nearby, eager to claim their babies at birth. In the first century some individuals were believed to have supernatural powers because they had a relationship with a demon "assistant" who carried out the spells they cast against others. Just who these evil spirits were and where they came from was a mystery. But no one doubted that they existed.

Today, as we have noted, our culture has seen a resurgence of paganism. And the many varieties of contemporary neopagans are quite fascinated by the spirit world. They worship "gods" and "goddesses" and view the spirit world as populated by a variety of heroes, spirits of the deceased, spirits awaiting birth, animal spirits and more, all of which are eager to help those currently living in this world. The ancients viewed the gods as selfish and capricious and unreliable at best. And they viewed all spirits as dangerous, for the spirits could be employed to gain control over another person or to do harm. The current new pagans view almost all spirits as benevolent, and so they approach the supernatural realm with confidence and expectation.

The four New Testament gospels picture Jesus interacting frequently with people who were afflicted by demons. These spirits were truly evil, causing blindness, deafness, crippling diseases and, in extreme cases, madness. In every confrontation Jesus commanded the demons to leave the person they were tormenting. And the demons, recognizing Jesus as the Son of God, were forced to obey. The people the demons oppressed were healed and freed.

The ancients puzzled over the nature and origin of evil spirits. The Bible answers the question, "What are demons?"

The Bible on Demons and Evil Spirits

Scripture tells us that before God created the material universe He created a host of spirit beings we call angels. But there was a rebellion among the angels, led by a powerful angel called Lucifer. The rebellion and Lucifer's motivation are described in Ezekiel 28:17 and Isaiah 14:12–14. The result of the rebellion was that Lucifer was transformed into Satan and the angels who followed him were transformed into demons. All were "cast down to the earth" (Isaiah 14:12). In Luke 10:18 Jesus tells His disciples, "I saw Satan fall like lightning from heaven," and in Matthew 25:41 Jesus refers to "the devil and his angels." What may be a graphic description of the epic battle precipitated by Satan's rebellion is found in Revelation 12:7–9:

> And there was war in heaven. Michael and his angels fought against the dragon, and the dragon and his angels fought back. But he was not strong enough, and they lost their place in heaven. The great dragon was hurled down—that ancient serpent called the devil, or Satan, who leads the whole world astray. He was hurled to the earth, and his angels with him.

Like Satan, the fallen angels who followed him—the demons, also called evil spirits—became the implacable enemies of God. And because God loves us, Satan and his demons seek to oppose God by oppressing and attacking human beings.

What is important for those of us who believe the Bible to realize is that there really is a spirit world lying alongside our material world. And according to Scripture, this spirit world is populated by just two kinds of beings: angels, spirits who love God and carry out His orders, and evil spirits, those who hate God and are committed to deceiving and tormenting human beings.

Scripture portrays a spirit world whose population can and does interact with our world. The Bible warns us against any attempt to contact that world, for the spirits there who are eager to reach us are evil. Whether the spirits take the form of ghosts or goddesses or masquerade as "spirit guides," underneath they are really demons.

Demons in Daily Life

"She just rubs me the wrong way," Tom told his wife. "I can't seem to help snapping back at her." Eileen nodded sympathetically. "I know what you mean. It's like Carol at church. We're on that committee together, but she's so bossy. And she doesn't want to hear any of my ideas. Next thing you know I'm getting angry and hostile. I've got to bite my tongue to keep from saying something nasty."

Pretty common? Absolutely. Life is filled with just such things. We have conflict with coworkers. We are tempted when we pass that bakery. (Just one pastry won't hurt, will it?) We promise ourselves to read the Bible more faithfully, but we turn on the TV instead. We get really irritated when our spouse starts to tell that story for the hundredth time.

We have learned to exercise care when it comes to labeling strange occurrences or someone's odd behavior automatically as demonic—we try not to see a demon under every bush. But sometimes we lean too far the other way. We never consider the possibility that demons might have something to do with the little things that mar our daily lives.

In our culture there are many far more rational explanations available to account for what happens in daily life. Conflict with a coworker? The reason is probably stress, or the fact that she is just an irritating individual. Frustrated at our failure to overcome a recurring temptation? Blame it on a lack of willpower or an eruption of the sin nature. Never seem to find time for prayer or reading the Bible? Our lives are just too busy, or we lack self-discipline. Growing distance in our marriages? Probably not getting enough sleep.

Such explanations do not help us resolve our conflicts, triumph over our temptations, spend more time with the Lord or deepen our love for those around us. But they do satisfy us. We have figured out what is wrong and feel no need to probe deeper. When there is a natural explanation, why look for a supernatural one? Why consider the possibility that the frustrations we experience in daily life have a spiritual root, and that evil spirits might be involved?

The Exorcist Effect

One reason we fail to consider demons is that our view of demonic activity has been shaped by movies like *The Exorcist*. We assume that when demons are involved all sorts of weird things happen. If we are not twisting and turning and throwing up or speaking in an eerie voice not our own, or if objects are not floating around the room, we never imagine supernatural involvement.

Too often deliverance ministers encourage this by expecting manifestations by the spirits they tell us they are casting out. A person has to drop writhing to the floor or faint with eyes rolling for demons to be involved. But is the bizarre really "the" mark of demonic activity? Do we honestly imagine that demons are all that eager to advertise their presence? If you were a demon, would you not more likely be intent on keeping your victims ignorant of your activity instead of putting on a show?

Which raises an important question. What should we expect from demons? What are possible indications that demons may be active in our daily lives?

In a very helpful book by Father Michael Scanlan and Randall Cirner, *Deliverance from Evil Spirits*, the authors suggest three primary ways that evil spirits affect humankind. They argue that evil spirits (1) tempt us, (2) oppose us and (3) seek to bring us into bondage. So if you are experiencing temptation, finding things going wrong in your life, or are in the grip of some habit or compulsion you cannot seem to break, the chances are that demons might be involved. In fact, it is in the little things that prevent us from the full experience of life in Christ that demons are most likely to be at work.

Evil Spirits and Temptation

Satan makes his first appearance in the Bible in Genesis 3, where he tempts Eve to violate God's command not to eat fruit from a particular tree. He subtly casts doubt on God's word and God's motives, leaving Eve to depend on her senses and on her best guess about the result of any choice she makes. The theme of temptation recurs through Scripture, and Jesus, who overcame temptations eerily reminiscent of Eve's (see Luke 4), warns us that His disciples can expect to experience severe temptations (see Luke 22:31).

Temptations are such an ordinary part of life that we hardly ever look at them as possible indications of demonic activity. Some temptations are little more than fleeting thoughts rejected immediately. Some temptations are recurrent, a pull toward an action we reject time and time again. Some temptations are overpowering, something we know we must reject but surrender to over and over until we despair of breaking the pattern of sin and repentance, only to sin again.

Demons can have a hand at every level of temptation, from the fleeting to the establishment of compulsive sinful behavior. Recognizing this reality provides us with an important resource to help us overcome temptations. This resource is the authority Jesus has given us to command demons in His name to stop their activity. Jesus' authority over demons is clearly demonstrated in the gospels. Every time Jesus came into contact with a demonized person—one who was in some way in bondage to one or more demons—Jesus commanded the demons to leave, and the demons were forced to obey.

The Bible makes it clear that Jesus gave His disciples authority over evil spirits. This means that we can command demons to leave or to cease specific activities. When we find ourselves tempted to respond in a sinful way in any situation, we can and should immediately command any demons involved to stop their activity or leave. It is certainly true that temptation is rooted in the response of our sin nature to various situations (see James 1:13–15). No command to a demon will affect our old nature's gravitation toward sin, but commanding in Jesus' name can limit demonic efforts to increase the intensity and frequency of our temptations.

A Question of Balance

How can we tell if we are dealing with demons, as opposed to natural liabilities of our—or someone else's—character? This is one of those questions for which there is no really good answer. The reason is that symptoms of demonization tend to mimic personality flaws, as well as physical and psychological illness. Confusing the issue even more, demons hitchhike on such conditions, exaggerating them and making them worse. Charles H. Kraft, who has an active and extensive deliverance ministry, gives the example that he has never counseled a wife beater whose fits of brutality did not have a demonic component, although the person might have always had difficulty controlling his temper.

Ultimately the only way to be sure that demons are present in our lives is to challenge them and force them to reveal themselves. By that I mean simply to speak directly to any demon who may be present and, in the name of Jesus, command the demon to reveal himself. This is not something you should pursue with another person who fears he or she may be demonized unless you have secured permission first. The demon should be directed to speak either within your mind or the mind of the other person you are helping, or to speak aloud using the human voice. A demon so challenged might not respond immediately, but anyone who is being demonized or harassed will sense the alien presence.

But then we face another question: How do we know if such challenges are warranted? It can be truly destructive to a person with a problem of natural causes to be treated as if he or she were demonized.

Recently I ran across helpful suggestions in a book entitled *Deliverance from Demons and Diseases* by Eric M. Hill (SunHill, 2004). He gives several examples of behaviors and thought patterns that people might have before and after demonic oppression. Before demonization, for instance, a person "has natural fears common to humanity"; after demonization, those "fears become tormenting or controlling." Before demonization, a person "has sin problems common to humanity"; after demonization, the person becomes a "slave to certain sins."

Since demons hitchhike on problems that stem from natural causes, hoping to exaggerate and intensify them, we can apply Hill's "before and after" line of thought to most any experience to help us diagnose possible demonic activity. For example:

It is normal to be self-conscious. *It may not be normal* to focus on imaginary flaws in one's looks or feel that one is constantly being judged.

It is normal to be subject to situational or chemical depression. *It may not be normal* when deep depression persists despite changes in situation or medication.

It is normal to develop habitual ways of doing things. *It may not be normal* when natural habits become compulsive and obsessive.

It is normal to have illness. *It may not be normal* when illnesses are chronic and do not respond to treatment.

It is normal to have difficulty concentrating when praying or reading the Bible. *It may not be normal* when these practices are constantly interrupted by evil thoughts, sleepiness or other distractions.

It is normal to have doubts about God's love or protection. *It may not be normal* when doubts become fears that cannot be resolved.

Particularly, when we see several patterns of behavior occurring together that seem to grow worse or have no resolution, it is worth our while to consider demonization.

It is not always easy to find the balance between, on one side, attributing every problem to demons and, on the other side, ignoring their existence, but we can learn to look for signs and symptoms that are good indicators. Is the problem most likely a personality quirk, phobia or mental illness? Or is the problem one of several that seem to indicate the destructive, intensifying presence of demons?

We should never dismiss the possibility of demonic activity. Too many pastors and Christian counselors never consider the fact that there is an invisible war going on, a struggle between good and true evil, a battle between angels and demons for the hearts and wills of human beings. Granted, it is seldom easy to diagnose demonization. But in our struggle of the world, the flesh and the devil, let's not ignore the devil.

The good news is that Jesus is far more powerful than evil spirits. The Son of God cast out demons in the first century, and He can free us from their influence today.

TO TALK ABOUT

1. How trustworthy do you consider descriptions of demonic activity in the gospels to be?
2. What does the fact tell you that in each confrontation with demons Jesus expelled them from the victim?
3. Are there any areas in your life you think of as natural in which it is possible that demons could be involved?

5

Interview with a Demon

Yesterday I gave my Sunday school class a quiz. I am going to start this chapter with a quiz, too. Actually, this quiz is easier. Simply read the verses listed below and identify a common element.

1. "When evening came, many who were [demonized] were brought to him, and he drove out the spirits with a word and healed all the sick" (Matthew 8:16).
2. "He also drove out many demons" (Mark 1:34).
3. "They [the disciples] drove out many demons" (Mark 6:13).
4. "Jesus was driving out a demon that was mute. When the demon left, the man who had been mute spoke, and the crowd was amazed" (Luke 11:14).
5. "Some Jews who went around driving out evil spirits tried to invoke the name of the Lord Jesus over those who were [demonized]" (Acts 19:13).

That is the quiz. Just five verses. Three of them are about what Jesus was doing, one about what the disciples were doing, and one about some Jewish exorcists who were trying to do the same thing. The common element is that each verse is about *driving out* demons, and there are many more verses I could have quoted.

What is fascinating about all of these verses is the phrase *driving out* or *drove out*. It is clear the demons did not want to go, but Jesus and later the disciples forced them to leave their victims. But the word I want to focus on is *out*. If demons were driven *out* of the demonized, the demons in some sense must have been *in* them. That is, individual demons established a presence within the personalities of the individuals they were oppressing. This raises an important question: How do demons gain entrance to a human being's personality and establish a presence there?

Doorways for Demons

The question of how demons gain entrance to a human's personality has no definitive answer. The reason is simple: The Bible does not deal with this question. When Jesus met a demonized individual, the demon was already there. Jesus dealt with the situation by exercising His authority and driving the evil spirit out.

While there is no biblical revelation on what constitutes doorways through which demons gain entrance to a person's life, those experienced in deliverance ministry generally recognize four primary doorways through which demons enter. These are trauma, trafficking with the occult, habitual personal sin and sins of the fathers.

Trauma

We often think of trauma as an intense, sudden, shattering experience that causes physical damage. But we need to realize that any wound that does substantial and lasting psychological damage is also trauma. The child whose parent is a perfectionist, always demanding more and more and never satisfied with the child's efforts, is enduring trauma that can persist into adulthood as a deep sense of inadequacy or self-condemnation. In the same way a child who is ignored by mom and dad can feel isolated and alone, an adult can need constant reassurance or become deeply depressed and discouraged. These kinds of deep emotional wounds provide footholds for demons, places where they can enter and claim they have a right to be present.

Demons who have established footholds in our lives through trauma are subject to Jesus, just as are other demons. Typically, however, there are several associated demons linked to psychological trauma: depression, discouragement, dejection, disappointment, despair, sadness, misery, gloom, hopelessness. . . . All are closely associated with psychological trauma. The challenge then is not simply to get one or two demons to stop oppressing the victim. Our challenge is to deal with a cluster of demons and to expel them. And we also need to deal with the trauma that created the foothold for the demons in the first place. The best book I have found identifying and dealing with associated groups of demons is Charles H. Kraft's *Two Hours to Freedom* (Chosen, 2010). I recommend this book to anyone interested in deliverance.

Later in this chapter I will introduce you to a young woman of our own time whose demonization probably began with trauma. We will look at her situation and in the process of her deliverance hear an "interview" with the demon who oppressed her.

Trafficking with the Occult

It is fascinating that so many who believe in a spirit world today assume that beings who inhabit it have only the best wishes for humankind. The curious often use Ouija boards to try to gain information from "the other side." Far more serious is the attempt to establish a personal relationship with a "spirit guide" in hope that the spirit will provide help and guidance for dealing with daily life issues. The danger in any kind of involvement with the occult is that the seeker will open a doorway into his or her life for an actual demon. And despite the naïveté of those involved with the occult, demons are always hostile to human beings.

This is why Scripture speaks so plainly to the issue in both Old and New Testaments. The definitive passage is found in Deuteronomy 18:10–12, which labels all occult practices as "detestable to the LORD."

> Let no one be found among you who sacrifices his son or daughter in the fire, who practices divination or sorcery, interprets omens, engages in witchcraft, or casts spells, or who is a medium or spiritist or who consults the dead. Anyone who does these things is detestable to the LORD.

While none of us can avoid a certain amount of trauma in our lives, we can certainly choose to avoid any and all contact with the occult.

Habitual Personal Sin

Repeated, unconfessed sin also seems to provide a doorway for demons. By *unconfessed* I mean both the failure to come to the Lord to acknowledge and repudiate our sin, and the failure to admit what we have done to a person we have sinned against. We should not make the mistake of identifying only certain "serious" sins as doorways. A fascination with pornography or repeated adultery certainly falls into the category of potential doorway sins, but so do bitterness and unforgiveness. God has given us a wonderful promise in 1 John 1:9: "If we confess our sins [acknowledge, take responsibility for], he is faithful and just and will forgive us our sins and purify us from all unrighteousness." Our sins and failures may open the door to demonization; following God's instruction and confessing our sins slams the door in the face of any demons.

Sins of the Fathers

It appears that some demons who are attached to individuals seem to transfer their influence to succeeding generations. While I disagree with the use of the following text to support generational transference, there are cases in which problems like those caused by demons do appear to run in families. Deuteronomy 5:9 says: "I, the Lord your God, am a jealous God, punishing the children for the sin of the fathers to the third and fourth generation of those who hate me." I discuss this more thoroughly in Part 2 of this book: "A Deliverance Dictionary." Please see the entry *Sins of the Fathers*.

Driving Out a Demon

While we have only general knowledge of what constitutes doorways for demons to enter and establish a presence in a person's life, we know much more about driving demons out. I want to illustrate this by quoting from a recorded exorcism.

C. Fred Dickason, whom I knew, was a longtime professor at Moody Bible Institute. He counseled many hundreds of students over his years there. Some four hundred of them gave signs that the problems they brought to Fred were caused by demons. Fred was forced to develop skills in identifying and dealing with the demons who were causing the students' problems. In time Fred began tape-recording some of the sessions with the students who came to him. In this chapter, I reproduce parts of a second counseling session with a young female student named Dottie.

We know very little about Dottie. From the recorded interview, portions of which Fred documented in his book, *Demon Possession and the Christian* (Moody Bible Institute, 1987), it seems that a demon entered Dottie's life before her conversion. The nature of the demon and his activity to cause confusion suggests that this demon entered through the doorway of trauma. While we do not know the exact situation that created the trauma, there are clues. It is likely that earlier in her life, probably in early childhood, something happened in her family—possibly a divorce or loss of a parent—that caused the young Dottie uncertainty and anxiety. The impact of the experience, exacerbated by the demon, resulted in a condition in which Dottie was unable to do her schoolwork and was struggling with uncertainty about whether or not she should be at Moody.

The excerpt begins at a point in the counseling session where a demon interrupts and addresses Fred directly, in a voice very different from Dottie's. In the segments below the demon's words are in italic.

> *"[We] don't like you because you tell too much, and you talk too much, and too many people are getting convinced!"*
> "Too many are getting convinced of what?"
> *"We have been at war with you for too doggone long, and we are sick of it!"*

"Who is 'we'?" [Demanding.]

"What do you mean, 'we'? You know who I am." [Angry.]

"What is your name?"

"Oh, come on! [Disgust.] You know my name. You named me. You named me last time I was here. You named me. You named me. So give me my name back!"

"No, you tell me your name."

"Oh, shut up!"

While demons have personal names, they normally tend to go by a description of what they are doing to their victims. After talking with the young student earlier, Fred was able to identify the demon tormenting her as Confusion. You can sense the demon's frustration at being so accurately named. Demons are slippery beings. Unless spoken to using the correct functional name, they often will pretend to obey but in fact ignore the commands you give in Jesus' name. We can sense the disgust in the demon Confusion. Fred has cut him off from a major route demons take to avoid obeying a believer performing an exorcism.

Prayer is a major resource believers have when dealing with demons. In this case the demon Confusion attempted to delay the exorcism, hoping to wait Fred out and hoping that Fred might overlook something that would keep him from being cast out. When Fred played the recording for me, I could hear the demon's voice clearly.

"You've only got a few more minutes, and I will wait it out."

Fred prayed that the Lord would put pressure on the demon and not allow any evasive action. The demon's response makes it clear that Jesus personally answered this prayer and intervened.

"Oh, no! No, no, no, no, not Jesus! Get away, get away, get away!"

"The Lord Jesus will not get away. He's inside of Dottie. [Prayer:] Lord Jesus, You are inside of Dottie; show Yourself to them in Your power, and cause them to stop this tormenting."

As the moment of the exorcism approaches, Fred forces the demon to admit not only that Christ has authority over him but that Dottie too has the authority to cast him out. In their earlier session Fred and Dottie both commanded Confusion and every demon under Confusion's authority to leave. This did not happen, and Fred wonders why. When questioned, the demon reveals why the first exorcism session failed to get the results Fred was looking for.

"Did you confess last time that Jesus Christ was your Victor?"
"Sure!"
"And that Dottie was your victor in Christ?"
"Sure."
"Did you tell her you would obey and leave?"
"Sure."
"When Jesus and Dottie agreed?"
"They haven't agreed yet."
"How do you know? Because you're not gone?"
"I'm interfering."

At this point Fred points out that Dottie is made in the image of God and is important to Him. The demon is still intent on arguing. Fred's response is to quote Scripture. It is impossible to over-emphasize the importance of memorizing Scripture. There will be many times when the Holy Spirit will guide to just the right verse to silence and maintain control over a demon. Here the demon responds to Fred's affirmation that Dottie is made in the image of God.

"Yes, but I put mud on it."

"Not so. The image has been restored. Ephesians 4:24 says that she has been re-created in righteousness and true holiness according to the image of God who created her. She is clean through the word that Christ has spoken to her."

"No! I'm in her body. That can't be."

We pick the tape up near the end.

"Confusion, I command you to leave by the authority of Christ."

"She was our princess!"

"She has been delivered from the kingdom of darkness into the Kingdom of God's dear Son."

After another shorter struggle, the demon admitted his defeat and left.

A Few Conclusions

As I point out in my book *Every Angel in the Bible* (Nelson, 2001), there are several conclusions we can draw from experiences of deliverance like this one. The first is that demons are real. They are personal beings who are active in the world today. Demons look for opportunities to gain access to human beings, where they will do what they can to disrupt our lives.

Demons are a defeated foe. Christ has authority over them. We believers can command demons in Jesus' name and force them to depart. Despite the fact that Christ is Lord, demons will use every trick they can think of to avoid being expelled. In the end, however, demons know they are defeated and doomed. They also know that believers have the authority to cast them out. Fred was persistent and refused to let the demon Confusion sidetrack him from his purpose. Fred also played Christian music to weaken the demon. Many passages of Scripture can be used in the same way.

While demonization should not be taken lightly, we can remain confident that Jesus Christ is Lord. We need the courage to expose and to confront any demons who may have entered the lives of believers.

TO TALK ABOUT

1. Can you think of any experiences in your life that could potentially have provided a doorway for demons?
2. If you suspected that a demon had some influence on you, would you be willing to undergo an exorcism? Why or why not?
3. Would you be willing to speak to a demon and cast it out? Would you be more willing if you were supported by several Christians praying as the exorcism was performed?

6

The Enemy, Up Close and Personal

In the last chapter I included portions of a transcript of a confrontation between Fred Dickason and a demon who had established a presence in a young Moody Bible Institute student. The demon was named Confusion, a name that reflected his influence on his young victim. Fred, acting with the authority that Jesus gives to believers, cast the demon out of the student.

It is fascinating that with so many references to demons and evil spirits in the gospels most Christians know so little about them. We know that the apostle Paul identifies "heavenly realms" as the abode of spirit beings. And we know that these beings, called rulers, authorities and "powers of this dark world" in the epistles are "spiritual forces of evil," against which believers are to stand (Ephesians 6:12). But nowhere in the New Testament are we told exactly what these spirit beings are or where they came from. Yet there is abundant evidence that enables us to establish their identity.

Part of the problem is caused by shifts in terminology. In the gospels the hostile spirit beings who oppress humans are called *demons* or *evil spirits*. We are used to thinking of them in these terms. Too many, however, noting these terms are not found outside the gospels, conclude that evil spirits are not really a concern of Christians today. In fact, both the Old Testament and the epistles have much to say to us about these hostile spirit beings who, like Satan himself, are our implacable enemies.

Old Testament Terminology

The key to understanding the role of evil spirits in the Old Testament is Deuteronomy 32:17, which reviews Israel's history and states: "They sacrificed to demons, which are not God—gods they had not known, gods that recently appeared, gods your fathers did not [know]." Moses is telling us that the "gods" worshiped by pagans in ancient times were in fact evil spirits, demons. The apostle Paul confirms this in 1 Corinthians 10:20, where he warns believers living in a pagan society that "the sacrifices of pagans are offered to demons, not to God."

Evil spirits have masqueraded as deities from the beginning, and evil spirits have been the powers behind every religion other than the one God has revealed in Scripture and in Jesus Christ. The terminology may differ. They might not be called *demons* or *evil spirits* in the sacred text. But Baal, Ashtoreth, Dagon and other deities worshiped by the peoples that surrounded Israel *were* demons. If we want to know what the Old Testament teaches about demons, all we need to do is explore the beliefs and practices associated with the deities of ancient peoples. There is abundant material in the Old Testament and in the literature of the ancients to help us understand the impact demons have had on human history and culture.

New Testament Terminology

A similar difference in terminology has led those who read the Bible today to assume that there is little or no mention of evil spirits in the epistles. This is because the supernatural beings called *demons* and *evil spirits* in the gospels, familiar terms to first-century Jews, were called by other names in the Hellenistic culture of the wider world.

In cities like Ephesus the supernatural beings were known by terms that conveyed the idea of power. Thus Paul writes that "our struggle is not against flesh and blood, but against the rulers, against the authorities, against the powers of this dark world and against the spiritual forces of evil in the heavenly realms" (Ephesians 6:12). Anyone reading these words in Paul's time would have known exactly what the apostle was saying. The believer is engaged in a cosmic struggle with evil supernatural beings. Although they are native to a different—a heavenly—realm, they have a dread impact on life "in this dark world." These rulers, authorities and powers included the deities the people worshiped, as well as other spirit beings.

Looking in the literature of the first century and inscriptions from that era, we understand the grip that fear of the supernatural beings had on men and women then. We can understand why the culture turned to magic (often spelled *magick* to distinguish occult practices from sleight-of-hand stage tricks) in a desperate attempt to manipulate the beings who were believed to exercise a malevolent influence on the lives of individuals.

When we understand these shifts in terminology we realize that the whole Bible, not just the gospels, speaks about evil spirits and their impact on human experience. The Old Testament may name them *gods*, but they are demons. New Testament letters may call them *authorities* and *powers*, but they are demons. Today neopagans may speak of *the goddess* or *the green man* and encourage others to welcome *spirit guides*, but by whatever name they are called, they are demons. We need to understand who they are, how they operate and the resources God has provided to enable us to stand against them.

The Origin of Demons: Two Theories

The apostle Paul portrays the heavenly realms as the abode of spirit beings. These rulers, authorities and "powers of this dark world" are the "spiritual forces of evil" against which believers must stand (Ephesians 6:12). The gospels are filled with references to demons who infect humans and cause various illnesses and difficulties. Clearly demons exist. But nowhere in the New Testament are we told exactly what the spirit beings are or where they came from.

In first-century Judaism there were two prevalent theories. The first was built on Isaiah 14 and Ezekiel 28, which were understood to describe the transformation of the angel Lucifer into the "prince of darkness." According to this theory, demons and evil spirits, which all ancient peoples believed populated the spirit world, were angels who had followed Satan in his great rebellion against the Creator.

The second theory was built on the Genesis 6 reference to *nephilim*, offspring of the "sons of God," understood to be angels, and human women. According to this second theory, demons are the disembodied spirits of these half-breeds who died in the subsequent Genesis flood.

No other theories were offered then or later. While in the first century the ghosts of humans were supposed to remain nearby for a time, and often supposed to harm the living, this was a pagan notion and not common in Judaism or early Christianity.

We are left, then, if we wish to be biblical in our search for the identity of evil spirits, to ask whether either of these ancient theories has additional support in Scripture. We discover very quickly that the second theory is given no additional support beyond the Genesis 6 passage from which it is drawn. But the theory that demons are fallen angels—angels who sided with Satan when he fell—does have considerable New Testament support. There are in fact five lines of evidence.

1. There is evidence that some angels fell with Satan. A statement in Revelation 12 pictures Satan as an "enormous red dragon" and refers to his tail sweeping "a third of the stars out of the sky and [flinging] them to earth" (verses 3–4). As angels are sometimes referred to in the Old Testament as "stars" (cf. Job 38:7), this reference is often taken as evidence that a third of the angels God created followed Satan in his rebellion. This interpretation is supported by Revelation 12:7, which describes "the dragon and his angels" at war with Michael and God's angels in heaven. A similar reference to the devil and his angels is found in Matthew 25:41.

2. There is evidence from parallel expressions. The "devil and his angels" are linked in Matthew 25:41 and Revelation 12:7. A parallel expression is found in Matthew 12:24, where reference is made to "Beelzebub [a name for Satan], the prince of

demons." In these expressions angels and demons are parallel, and thus arguably the same.

3. There is evidence from parallel activities. The Bible pictures demons as seeking to enter and control individuals (see Matthew 17:14–18; Luke 11:14–15), something that Satan also does (see Luke 22:3; 1 John 3:12). In the same way evil angels are seen joining Satan to war against God, just as are demons (see Mark 9:17–27; Revelation 9:1).

4. There is evidence from essential being. Angels are called "spirits" in Psalm 104:4 (AKJV) and Hebrews 1:14. Demons are also called "spirits" (see Matthew 8:16; Luke 4:36).

5. There is evidence from personhood. Both angels and demons are referred to by personal pronouns, indicating that both are personal beings (see Luke 8:30). While members of a class, both angels and demons are revealed to be individuals. Like angels, demons can communicate with us and are pictured as having emotions, intelligence and other marks of personhood (see Luke 8:31). As above, angels and demons are pictured as individuals in Scripture.

While any one of these points might be challenged, it is difficult to imagine that five distinct lines of evidence, each of which supports the same theory, are likely to lead to an erroneous conclusion. In short, there is enough scriptural evidence to conclude with confidence that the demons of the gospels and the powers of the epistles are in fact angels who rebelled against God and fell with Satan.

Whatever their origins, there clearly are supernatural beings who are engaged with Satan in an invisible war against God and humankind. The good news is that Satan and his followers are defeated foes, and as we follow Scripture's guidelines we can meet and defeat them today.

Secondhand Exorcism

Certain first-century pagan and Jewish beliefs coincided with the teachings of the Old Testament. There was agreement that demons seek to be worshiped as gods. There was agreement that demons are deeply involved in occult practices. There was also agreement that demons are basically hostile to human beings and eager to do us harm. Many pagan and Jewish beliefs, however, are not reflected in the Old or New Testaments.

Neither first-century pagans nor first-century Jews had any doubt about the ability of demons to trouble human beings. Stories of demonic possession and oppression are found in the New Testament. Similar stories are common in Jewish and pagan literature of the period as well.

It is not surprising that the widespread experience of what was believed to be demonic oppression or possession was matched by an equally widespread belief in exorcism. General opinion held that learning a demon's name gave a human some control over the evil spirit and its powers. This belief was the foundation of exorcism. This is illustrated by the following Jewish incantation against boils, quoted by Alfred Edersheim in *The Life and Times of Jesus the Messiah* (Longmans, 1900):

> Baz, Basiya, Mas, Masiya, Kas, Kasiyah, Shalia and Marlai—ye angels that come from the land of Sodom to heal painful boils! Let the color not become more red, let it not further spread, let it seed to be absorbed in the belly. As a mule does not propagate

itself, so let not this evil propagate itself in the body of [name], son of [name].

Jewish Exorcists

I mentioned earlier that Jewish exorcists were particularly prized by pagans. They had heard that the Jews had access to the secret name of their God, who was thought to be particularly powerful. Against this background, we can understand how one family of Jewish exorcists felt when Paul showed up in Ephesus and did "extraordinary miracles," including healing the demonized and driving out "evil spirits" (Acts 19:11–12). They responded by trying to use the name of Jesus in a magical way:

> Some Jews who went around driving out evil spirits tried to invoke the name of the Lord Jesus over those who were [demonized]. They would say, "In the name of Jesus, whom Paul preaches, I command you to come out." Seven sons of Sceva, a Jewish chief priest, were doing this. One day the evil spirit answered them, "Jesus I know, and I know about Paul, but who are you?" Then the man who had the evil spirit jumped on them and overpowered them all. He gave them such a beating that they ran out of the house naked and bleeding.
>
> Acts 19:13–16

The seven sons of Sceva practiced secondhand exorcism. That is, they used the name of Jesus as if that name had magical powers, without knowing Jesus. They failed to realize that only someone who has a personal relationship with Jesus, and thus a right to call on Him, can perform an exorcism in Jesus' name.

The name *Jesus Christ* does not have magical power. Saying the name does not give anyone magical ability. But the person who trusts Jesus as Savior and thus has established a personal relationship with Him can call on Jesus to act. It is Jesus, God the Son, the living Person who has authority over all His creation, who drives out demons. And Jesus is the only one who can.

Exorcism Today

The evil spirits the Bible speaks about are real. And evil spirits—demons—have powers and abilities that we cannot understand or match. Demons are a real danger to any person who knowingly or unknowingly opens himself up to demonization. Whether a person approaches the demonic out of curiosity or in the hope of manipulating the spirit world or for some other reason, that person places him or herself in grave danger.

At the same time, we are to remember that Jesus gave His followers the authority to cast demons out of those who are demonized. This authority was not given just to the twelve apostles, although they were the first to be empowered (see Mark 3:15). Jesus later gave that same authority to 72 ordinary followers who are identified only as "workers." While reporting back on their experiences, the 72 were excited that "even the demons submit to us in your name" (Luke 10:17). Jesus seems to have minimized this experience, telling the 72, "I have given you authority . . . to overcome all the power of the enemy." But He added, "Do not rejoice that the spirits submit to you, but rejoice that your names are written in heaven" (Luke 10:19–20).

Our authority over demons is limited. We are not authorized to use or manipulate the demonic. We are not authorized to question them about their realm.

Scripture reveals all that God has determined is necessary for us to know about demons. What believers *are* authorized to do is in Jesus' name drive demons out of those who are demonized. This gift of God is enough. We do not need to know more about the realm of Satan and his angels. All we need to know when presented with one of Satan's victims is how to drive out the evil spirit and give our brother or sister the gift of freedom.

While the Bible does not record other instances of ordinary Christians (or the Twelve) driving out demons, exorcisms are documented in Acts 5:16 and 19:11–12. The writings of the early Church fathers treat exorcism as rather commonplace in the early centuries of the Christian era. In a culture where evil spirits were commonly viewed and experienced as supernatural powers, the ability of Christians to drive out demons in the name of Jesus made a great impression on the population. In our world, exorcism is dismissed by most—even by committed Christians—as a fantasy. Yet demons are real, and the authority to cast them out of victims remains an important gift God has given to His people.

TO TALK ABOUT

1. Do you think it is important to know what demons and evil spirits are? Why or why not?
2. Why do you suppose our authority over evil spirits is limited to driving them out?
3. What reasons can you think of that might explain the lack of awareness in our day of the activities of demons?

7

Just Go Away

Demons, like the demon Confusion who had established a presence in the student I wrote about in chapter 5, look for opportunities to attach themselves to Christians. Never doubt that there are evil spirits looking eagerly for an opportunity to enter your life in order to corrupt you and your relationships with others.

This does not, however, mean that you or I have to let the demons in. A friend of mine who is a Christian counselor called me about her nine-year-old daughter. It seems that when her daughter went to bed at night, the little girl could sense someone or something probing about the room and calling her name. This was especially disturbing since her much loved grandfather had recently died. The repeated experiences frightened the girl, and she began to resist going to bed.

"What's happening?" the mother asked.

When her daughter explained, the mother called me. "What can I do about it?"

I took what the mother told me seriously. It might have been that a demon, taking advantage of trauma caused by the grandfather's death, was seeking to establish a foothold in the girl's life. My suggestion was simple. The mother and her daughter are members of a strong Christian family I have known for many years. I suggested she tell her daughter that whenever she heard that voice or sensed something coming near, she order it in the name of Jesus to go away and not come back.

The daughter was relieved to know what to do. Later I learned that the visitations continued for several nights, but each time the girl commanded the spirit in the name of Jesus to leave. When she did the voice seemed weaker and further away. After about a week the visitations ended, and the voice has not been heard since.

Unfortunately, most efforts by demons to establish a presence in a person's life are not as apparent or thwarted as easily as this one was. Thankfully, though, even demons who have successfully settled in can be thrown out.

Exorcism

Put simply, exorcism is the process of casting a demon (an evil spirit) out of a person in whom the demon has established a presence. In most cases this need not be a lengthy process, as Kraft explains in his excellent book *Two Hours to Freedom*. In other cases, as in the case of the student reported in chapter 5, it may take two or more sessions. In either case, there are certain things to which one needs to be sensitive. In this chapter I will describe a step-by-step process. Each step might be accomplished quickly or might take more time. The steps are:

1. Raise the possibility of demonization
2. Obtain permission and explain the process
3. Establish your authority
4. Identify any demon(s) present
5. Expel the demon(s)
6. Establish protection

Raise the Possibility of Demonization

I received an email from a mom in Texas. She told me her twenty-year-old son had been acting strangely, and she feared that demons were behind what was happening. Her son had always been outgoing and gregarious. But in the previous six months he had changed radically. Once a friendly and open individual, he had become hostile and reclusive, spending most of his time alone in his room and abandoning his circle of friends. The family simply could not recognize him as the person they had known all their lives.

I asked the mother if she was aware of anything upsetting that had happened to her son just before he changed. No, nothing she was aware of.

I asked if she had tried to talk with her son about what was happening. She had tried, but he insisted he had not changed.

In this particular case I suggested confrontation. Sit down with the son and with other family members who shared her concern. Relate what they were experiencing with him. Tell him that they were worried about him, and ask if anything had happened to bring about the changes they observed in him.

The son reacted to their intervention with hostility and anger. He insisted he had not changed. He was the same. And, if he was different, it was the fault of the mom and the rest of the family.

To the mom it felt as though the intervention had been a failure. But, assuming that the son really was not aware of how he had changed or of an experience that had triggered the change, the intervention established several things. First, the family was convinced that the son was acting strangely. He might have been aware of this before the intervention, but now he had additional evidence that he really had changed. Second, there was the possibility that the changes the family identified were not the son's fault. No one was blaming him. And third, if there were no identifiable natural causes for his changes in attitude and behavior, there was the possibility of a demonic cause. Nothing had been settled by the intervention. But the possibility of demonization was now established.

Unlike the son in this story, most individuals are aware that they have significant problems. Too many find themselves drawn to pornography, though they feel ashamed and try to resist. Others regularly lose their tempers and strike out at family members. Others feel anxious and fearful without any particular reason. Some experience chronic physical problems that the doctors cannot diagnose and that fail to respond to treatment. Others are successful in their work, but find themselves overwhelmed at times by doubt and uncertainty. Such experiences as these are disturbing, especially if they occur again and again. While there may be natural causes for such things, each of these could also have a demonic root.

If a friend mentions a problem, for instance, there is nothing wrong with asking, "Have you considered the possibility that it might not be your fault? That evil spirits or demons might be the cause?"

This is likely to be a totally new thought, whether or not the friend believes in demons. Make it clear that you are not saying demons *are* involved but are simply raising the possibility. Also make it clear that there are ways to find out if the problem has a supernatural cause.

Obtain Permission and Explain the Process

Most Christians might be willing to consider the possibility of a demonic cause of their problems. Few, however, will understand the process of exorcism. It is important to establish the fact that Christians can cast out evil spirits today. The friend can then make the decision whether or not to go forward with the exorcism.

Most people in our culture know that Jesus cast evil spirits out of those who were demonized in His day. But even Christians might not realize that Christ gave believers authority to drive out demons. If you have a Bible handy, you might want to share key verses from the gospels. As an option, I suggest memorizing parts of verses (see samples following) in case you ever deal with anyone who is demonized. Together these verses, with others, provide unmistakable evidence that Jesus' followers as well as Christ Himself can drive out demons.

Mark 3:14–15, for instance, says that Jesus "appointed twelve— designating them apostles—that they might be with him and that he might send them out to preach and to have authority to drive out demons." And Mark 16:17 promises that "those who believe" in Jesus "will drive out demons." If there is a demonic root to problems we experience, the demons causing the problems really can be driven out.

At this point you might ask your friend: "If it were demons, would you like to find that out and get rid of them?"

Surprisingly, many people do not want to know. Like the pastor I mentioned in an earlier chapter, they would rather continue to lose their tempers or be anxious and fearful than even to consider the possibility of demons. We have to respect the wishes of folks like this and let the matter drop. It may be that the person will think about the possibility of demons and raise the subject later. At any rate, the only thing you can do for someone who does not want to consider the possibility of demonization is to pray that, if demons are involved, he or she will bring the subject up again. And that you can then encourage him or her to consider an exorcism.

If your friend wishes to continue, share something of the process. Explain that the first thing you will try to do is identify any demons present by name. You can say that demons have names that are linked to the problems they cause—for instance, a demon who exaggerates a person's fears might be named Fear, Anxiety or, depending on the intensity of the fear, Terror. A demon who exaggerates an individual's sense of hopelessness might be named Hopelessness, Despair or Depression.

Tell your friend that you will proceed simply by talking with him or her. Also explain that you expect the demon(s) to communicate with you. Your friend can choose to give the demon(s) permission to use his or her voice and speak out loud. This is what happened in the exorcism included in chapter 5. Otherwise the demon(s) can respond within the victim. The person will sense the demon's response, whether the demon uses words or communicates wordlessly. In my experience communication is generally to and within the person, who then tells me what is happening.

Tell your friend that once you have identified any demons present by their names, you will then address those demons directly and command them to leave.

Also mention to your friend that following a successful exorcism, he or she is likely to feel a great sense of relief and will be aware that something evil has left. With the evil spirit(s) cast out, you will then explore together how the person can keep demons from returning.

Establish Your Authority

Now speak directly to any evil spirits who may be present in the victim. Remind the demons that you are speaking to the spirit world in the name of Jesus and with His authority. I find it helpful to remind any demons present of just who Jesus is and of His supreme authority. Reading a passage like Ephesians 1:19–23 does just this. It also makes clear that you know everything has been "placed under His feet," including the spirit world and its inhabitants of angels and demons. It is in the name of Jesus and with His authority that you cast out demons.

Identify Any Demon(s) Present

While demons sometimes have personal names, they also go by the name of the response they cause in the demonized person. In the case reported in chapter 5, Fred Dickason identified a demon named Confusion.

Demons seem to be quite legalistic, so it is important to name any evil spirits who are troubling an individual. If we do not address evil spirits by name, they seem to feel free to lie and try to deceive us. This is the significance of the interaction between Dickason and the demon Confusion.

The response of a victim to the evil spirit's influence provides clues to its name. If the person reports feelings of anxiety, the demon might go by Anxiety or by a synonym such as Worry or Fear. Command the demon in Jesus' name to confirm its name.

When more than one demon is present, one of them will be the lead demon. When you have contacted any demon, command it to name any other evil spirits that are present in the person and also to provide the name of the lead demon. This is likely to be resisted, as the lead (more powerful) demon will be countering your commands with commands of its own. One of my friends, when facing this situation, in the name of Jesus commands any demons other than the one he has identified and is speaking to not to hear what he is saying.

Demons definitely will not want to reveal their names. This command might need to be repeated several times before a reluctant spirit acknowledges its name. But once the name of the demon has been established, you can go ahead with the exorcism. From this point it is best to speak directly to the lead demon.

Expel the Demon(s)

Exorcism is a power encounter in which the demon has no chance of winning. It is important to approach an exorcism with this conviction. Some demons are stronger and more powerful than others, but no demon can successfully resist the power of Jesus. It is important for you to understand that you deal with demons only in the power and authority Jesus gives you as a believer. You will want to be clear when you speak to any evil spirits that you are relying completely on Jesus and commanding them in His name.

There is one other thing to remember. Scripture tells us that Jesus gives His followers authority to "cast out" demons. I believe this is a limited authority. That is, Christ did not give anyone authority to question demons about their realm. Certainly Christ gave us no authority to attempt to use demons in any way. We have no authority at all to satisfy our curiosity about the spirit world. What we do have is the authority to cast demons out of a person in whom they have established a presence and to free that individual from demonic influence.

When the identity of the demons present has been established, you can command them in the name of Jesus to leave. The actual act of exorcism is quite simple. You speak directly to a resident demon, using its name, and command it in the name of Jesus to leave the demonized person. The command can be repeated if the demon resists. You have authority granted by Jesus to cast evil spirits out, and in the end no demon can resist Christ.

Since it is not unusual for more than one evil spirit to have taken up residence in an individual, it is important to take steps to rid the victim of all the spirits present. Many of my friends, when helping a demonized person, will deal with all of the demons present as a group, using imagery in the command to leave. You might, for instance, require the lead spirit to chain together all the spirits present. Or you might command all the spirits to get into a box and close the lid. You then command the chained or boxed spirits as a group to report to Jesus for whatever disposal He chooses.

Establish Protection

Luke 11:24–26 provides an important reminder to anyone performing an exorcism. Casting evil spirits out of a person should not be the end of the ministry.

"When an evil spirit comes out of a man, it goes through arid places seeking rest and does not find it. Then it says, 'I will return to the house I left.' When it arrives, it finds the house swept clean and put in order. Then it goes and takes seven other spirits more wicked than itself, and they go in and live there. And the final condition of that man is worse than the first."

In this story told by Jesus, it seems that a person who has been demonized holds a special attraction for any spirits who had taken up residence there. The possibility always exists that demons might attempt to return.

One person I know who performs exorcisms always adds these words to the command to leave: "And don't come back." I cannot fault this. But I am not sure if our authority to cast out demons extends to commanding them not to return.

What is more significant is Jesus' description of the "house swept clean and put in order" but apparently empty. If we leave the exorcised individual with an empty "house," he or she will have no protection against re-demonization.

In the next chapter we will take a look at what believers can do to prevent either initial or recurrent demonization.

TO TALK ABOUT

1. What are several Bible passages that you might read or quote that emphasize who Jesus is and His authority?
2. Do you know anyone you suspect might be demonized? What makes you suspicious?
3. Would you be willing to attempt an exorcism if you suspected that a friend or loved one was demonized?

8

Knock, Knock

Jesus told the story of a man who had been freed from an evil spirit. The story, given from the point of view of the demon, is found in Matthew 12:43–45.

> "When an evil spirit comes out of a man, it goes through arid places seeking rest and does not find it. Then it says, 'I will return to the house I left.' When it arrives, it finds the house unoccupied, swept clean and put in order. Then it goes and takes with it seven other spirits more wicked than itself, and they go in and live there. And the final condition of that man is worse than the first."

This story is a strong reminder that casting an evil spirit out of a person should not be the end of our ministry. We need to stay with that individual, support and encourage him or her, and establish protection, because the spirits certainly will come back knocking on the door.

A friend of mine, a young Chinese-American businessman, was infected with the spirit of pornography. Even after the demon had been cast out, he found himself terribly tempted to return to the pictures that had dominated his life for over two years. Earlier he had confessed his sin to his wife as well as two Christian friends. Now those two friends came alongside him and at regular weekly lunches questioned how he was doing and held him accountable. With their help, he was able to reestablish an intimate relationship with Christ, gradually overcome his lust and hold off the spirit that had kept him in bondage.

There are several things about his experience that are significant. He was a believer, but as his addiction grew his connection with Jesus became weaker and weaker. He was truly, in the words of Jesus, "unoccupied." But then, after the demon was cast out, with his wife's support his friends also came alongside him. They encouraged him to grow spiritually, and they held him accountable for any slip. As he shared his life with these two brothers, his commitment to Jesus grew, and he gradually overcame the temptation entirely, blocking any return of the evil spirit.

It truly is important to follow up after exorcism. But it is just as important to close off the avenues through which demons enter in the first place. In chapter 5 I noted that those involved in deliverance ministry typically identify four major avenues through which demons commonly find access to a person's life. These avenues are trafficking with the occult, habitual personal sin, trauma and sins of the fathers. In this chapter we look at some of the ways a person can protect himself or herself from demonization, whether an original infestation or an attempt by demons who have been cast out to return.

Trafficking with the Occult

The Christian Answers Network website notes that "the word 'occult' is generally associated with secret knowledge and with practices dealing with the supernatural, often for the purpose of obtaining personal power." The site also observes that "occultism is rapidly increasing throughout the world." There are now thousands of publishers of occult books and magazines. Many of these are readily available on the Internet for little or no cost.

Deuteronomy 18:10–12 forbids occult practices common among peoples of the ancient Middle East. The text reads:

> Let no one be found among you who . . . practices divination or sorcery, interprets omens, engages in witchcraft, or casts spells, or who is a medium or spiritist or who consults the dead. Anyone who does these things is detestable to the LORD.

We can add to this list a number of occult practices that are common in our day: astrology, automatic speaking or writing, channeling, fortune-telling, horoscopes, incantations, Ouija boards, magick, shamanism, casting spells, spirit guides, tarot cards, tea reading, Wicca, witchcraft and others. Today it seems almost impossible to eliminate completely any contact with the occult. On just one day's schedule of DirecTV programming I found more than 25 shows based on the supernatural or paranormal.

What we often overlook is the fact that, to some extent, occult practices "work." We see this in a story recorded in Exodus 7. God has sent Moses to Pharaoh to demand that the Egyptian ruler release the Israelite slaves. He has also given Moses authority to perform a miraculous sign: When Pharaoh challenges Moses to perform a miracle, Moses is to tell Aaron to take his staff, "throw it down before Pharaoh, and it will become a snake" (verse 9). This occurred just as God had spoken.

Rather than be convinced, however, "Pharaoh then summoned wise men and sorcerers, and the Egyptian magicians also did the same things by their secret arts" (verse 11). The fact that the snake that had been Aaron's staff "swallowed up" the snakes fashioned from the Egyptians' staffs apparently made little impression on Pharaoh.

Yes, to some extent, occult practices actually do "work." Demons have real powers and can affect events in our world. I know more than one person who claims that the "spirit guides" he or she asked for and received helped significantly in making decisions that turned out well. I am not surprised. Satan's agents are more than happy to trade a few minor gifts in exchange for a person's unawareness of his need for a personal relationship with God.

Calling on the occult for guidance or help may seem to produce positive results for some. Yet dabbling in the occult in any form is "detestable to the Lord" for many reasons, not least of which might be its potential to bring His children into contact with the real evil spirits lurking beneath these practices—spirits who are eager to enter our lives, blind us to spiritual truth and ultimately lead us into misery and destruction.

To protect ourselves from initial infestation or re-infestation by evil spirits, we need to ensure that we avoid any and all contact with the occult. That woman reading tea leaves in the little restaurant in the shopping center might be totally harmless. But her connection to the occult could be real, and visiting her could open you to demonization. That TV program featuring the paranormal might only be entertainment, but watching it could make you more open to admitting an evil spirit into your life. It is vital for any person who wants to close the door to the entry of evil spirits to have nothing to do with the occult.

Habitual Personal Sin

The apostle James reminds us, "We all stumble in many ways" (James 3:2). First John provides God's remedy: "If we confess our sins, he is faithful and just and will forgive us our sins and purify us from all unrighteousness" (1 John 1:9). The tense of the verb here indicates progressive action: He will "keep on purifying us" from all unrighteousness. For this purifying process to take place we need to become aware of our sins and acknowledge them to God (and often to others). We can count on the Holy Spirit's help to repudiate confessed sins and enable us to live progressively righteous lives.

All too often we do not recognize our sins and so fail to confess them. Scripture calls this self-deception, and warns against Satan, who "[goes] out to deceive" (Revelation 20:8). Jesus said to His disciples, "When anyone hears the message about the kingdom and does not understand it, the evil one comes and snatches away what was sown in his heart" (Matthew 13:19).

I learned this lesson the hard way. Early in our marriage, I lied to my second wife about financial help I was providing my adult children from the first marriage. Even though I finally confessed what I had done, I continued to deceive her in little ways. Gradually I began to blame her for her reactions and became dismissive. I told myself that she reacted too strongly, and so I had to keep some things a secret from her. Even though I believe strongly in equality in marriage, I treated her less and less as a full partner. She recognized my attitude and was deeply hurt. It is hardly necessary to say that my actions and my attitude affected our relationship significantly and made it fall far short of what it could have been had I been honest and respected her as a full partner.

I cannot say that it was Satan who deceived me and shaped my attitude. I have to take full responsibility for what I did. I certainly was deceiving myself. Yet one of Satan's strategies is to deceive and to encourage our self-deception. My sin had become habitual, and it opened the door for the devil to influence my life.

It may seem strange that Scripture associates Satan with the more "common" sins like immorality or an angry attitude—as opposed to actions we would consider to be more serious or evil crimes, like rape or murder. In his letters to the Corinthians, Paul writes about a brother who had sinned sexually and had been disciplined by the Christian community (see 1 Corinthians 5). The disciplined man had repented and changed his ways, but the church was still inflicting punishment on him. Paul wrote and urged them to forgive "in order that Satan might not outwit us" (2 Corinthians 2:11). Paul added, "For we are not unaware of his schemes" (verse 11). There is a similar passage in Ephesians. There the apostle Paul says, "'In your anger do not sin.' Do not let the sun go down while you are still angry, and do not give the devil a foothold" (Ephesians 4:26–27).

There are no similar passages that link demons to violent, hate-filled actions. I suspect the reason is that, just as I was unaware for so long of my sin against my wife, most of us pass off sins like unforgiveness and anger as insignificant. Yet these are the very things that "give the devil a foothold."

What should we do to close such doorways to demonic entry? Not surprisingly, the New Testament says quite a lot about forgiveness. It also contains significant warnings against anger. And it speaks powerfully about how husbands are to love their wives. In almost any of the epistles there are exhortations to godly living that deal with what we might call commonplace morality. It is failure in these areas that is the most likely entry point for demons.

What can we do to protect ourselves? A key passage is found in the book of James, where the apostle is warning against anger:

> Do not merely listen to the word, and so deceive yourselves. Do what it says. Anyone who listens to the word but does not do what it says is like a man who looks at his face in a mirror and, after looking at himself, goes away and immediately forgets what he looks like. But the man who looks intently into the perfect law that gives freedom, and continues to do this, not forgetting what he has heard, but doing it—he will be blessed in what he does.
>
> James 1:22–25

The secret to protecting ourselves from those seemingly little sins that open us to demonization is contained in this James passage. We are to look into Scripture, use it as a mirror to help us see ourselves more clearly, and put what we find there into practice. God's Word, searched for guidance in everyday living and used to see ourselves and our actions from His perspective, will reveal our flaws. Then, not forgetting what we have seen of ourselves and of God's ways, we are to commit to living life God's way.

This is a far more personal and rigorous way to search the Scriptures than devotional reading or even "Bible study." It calls for us to be open about our lives and to engage in serious self-examination. We are always in danger of self-deceit. As James says, we must use Scripture as a mirror to see our true selves, recognizing what we need to do and then "doing it."

Trauma

Most of those involved in deliverance ministry, and most authors who write about it, identify trauma as a major entry point for demons. Unfortunately, almost no one explains how the traumas we experience provide access to demons. One exception to this is author and minister Peter Horrobin. In a concise treatment of the subject of trauma, included as a chapter in Doris Wagner's *How to Minister Freedom* (Regal, 2005), Horrobin points out that human beings have a physical nature, a psychological nature and a spiritual nature. We are more than our bodies. We are body, soul and spirit.

Horrobin explains that whether traumas are psychological (that is, mental) or physical, the whole person can be affected. It is not unusual for psychological trauma to express itself in physical symptoms. Nor is it surprising for significant physical injury to have equally significant psychological implications. But what actually are traumas, or in ordinary speech, hurts?

The child who is ridiculed in front of his schoolmates by the teacher is experiencing trauma. In some boys and girls this hurt is momentary and shrugged off. In more sensitive children, the trauma might have lasting impact and find expression later in life. It could surface as unwillingness to speak up for fear of making a mistake or an inability to trust authority figures. The young girl who is laughed at because of the early development of her figure might respond to the hurt with shame and self-rejection. A person severely injured in a car accident could find himself plagued by unexplained fears of the future. His confidence is gone, and he lives constantly on edge. The parents who receive unexpected news of their child's death might again and again relive the horror as at unexpected moments life triggers a recurrence of their emotions.

In the same way we sometimes experience spiritual trauma. A child has been taught that God answers prayer. When she prays for a much-loved grandmother to get well, and the grandmother dies, it can have a traumatic impact on the child. One older man

I know, when he was a child, went to the kitchen at a church pot-luck supper to ask for a particular slice of cake. He was told the cake was gone. But later he saw women in the kitchen eating that very cake. He told me that he was now more than seventy years old and had never been inside a church since that day. If that was how Christians acted, he wanted nothing to do with them. Disappointment, unanswered prayer, a decision to obey God that ends disastrously—all can be experienced as trauma, especially by new or untaught believers.

Each of these things is a trauma or hurt. It is probably clearer for us if we think of *trauma* as "anything that hurts us in any aspect of our being: physical, spiritual or psychological." None of us is free from trauma. We all will experience hurts as we live our lives. A peculiar thing about trauma, however, is that individuals tend to respond differently to what are essentially the same hurts. For one child, the pain of being yelled at by a parent has lasting and tragic effects. For another child, that experience brings a feeling of anger with a flash of resentment but has no lasting impact.

Whether or not a trauma—a hurt—opens the door for a demonic entry, any long-term impact on the person's life seems to be keyed to emotions. Hurts are often associated with fear, with anger, with shame, even with self-loathing. Under the stress caused by the hurt, normal defenses are breached as we experience inner chaos and our emotions run riot. It is this, our powerful emotional reaction, that seems to provide access to demons.

Earlier we noted that demons go by their functional names. That is, while demons can have personal names, we identify a demon who is oppressing or occupying a believer by the reaction the demon is causing or enhancing in the individual. Thus, the demon in chapter 5 was named Confusion because he intensified confusion in the young woman he had accessed. We find the same thing in the demons who gain access through trauma. They will be demons tuned specifically to the reaction of the victim to his or her trauma. If that reaction was fear, demon Fear will find an access point. If that reaction was bitterness, demon Bitterness or demon Unforgiveness will attach himself to the emotion and find a way into the individual's life.

When we understand that it is the emotional response to the hurt and the intensity of that emotional response that provides access to demons, we can see why traumas are such common avenues to demonization.

First Peter 5:6–9 provides insight. This passage is closely linked to our experience of trauma:

> Humble yourselves, therefore, under God's mighty hand, that he may lift you up in due time. Cast all your anxiety on him because he cares for you. Be self-controlled and alert. Your enemy the devil prowls around like a roaring lion looking for someone to devour. Resist him, standing firm in the faith, because you know that your brothers throughout the world are undergoing the same kind of sufferings.

It is only natural when we experience trauma that our emotions surge. It is only natural that we experience momentary doubts and fears. The solution is to humble ourselves under God's mighty hand. We were hurt, yet God remains in charge. And His goal is to lift us up. That is why we are able to cast all our anxiety on Him. Satan roars, an image reminding us that he is eager to devour us. But even in trauma we can stand firm in our faith, because we know the loving nature of God and that the Father is committed to us as His children.

This can be difficult for a young child who experiences trauma to understand. What such a child will understand, as we wrap our loving arms around her and reassure her both of our love and of God's love, is that despite the pain, she is safe in God's care.

How can we free ourselves from the demons of trauma and their effects on our personality?

A skilled deliverance minister can help a victim identify the original incident or incidents. Often the deliverance minister will then encourage the victim to visualize where Jesus is and what Jesus is doing while the trauma was being experienced. When this visualization is effective, a victim is likely to say something like "He's weeping" or "He has His hand on my shoulder and looks concerned." At that point the deliverance minister might tell the victim to envision taking the anxiety and giving it to Jesus.

Something like this process has provided a sense of freedom for many who were experiencing demonic oppression. It is important, however, not to stop at this point. The next step is to forgive the person or persons who caused the hurt. This expression of forgiveness will go a long way in confirming any healing that has been taking place and open the door to even more healing.

If you have experienced any trauma that affects your daily living but do not have access to a reputable deliverance minister, you can still get help. Share your pain with a trusted pastor or spiritually mature friend. Your prayer time together and the heartfelt expression of forgiveness toward those who hurt you will help you identify and close the doors to demons that have attached to your emotions through the pain you have suffered.

Sins of the Fathers

Deliverance ministers have observed often that certain problems they associate with demonization seem to run in families. This has led to the topic of generational demonization—that is, in some way some demons gain access to a person through that person's relationship with parents, grandparents, etc. Because this is such a widely accepted idea, I provide an extended analysis and evaluation of it in Part 2 of this book: "A Deliverance Dictionary." Please see the entry *Sins of the Fathers*.

TO TALK ABOUT

1. Through which of the avenues discussed in this chapter do you feel most vulnerable to demonization?
2. What have you done to guard yourself from demonization?
3. How important do you think sharing your problems with other Christians would be if you had experienced or were looking for deliverance from demonization?

9

Soul and Culture

We are used to thinking of the activity of demons, evil angels, in terms of their impact on individuals. This is understandable. The gospels focus on stories of those who were oppressed by demons whom Jesus subsequently confronted and cast out. But Satan does not concentrate all of his efforts in attacks on individuals. There is a story in the book of Daniel that gives us insight into Satan's broader schemes. Satan is not only interested in keeping individuals in bondage; Satan is also deeply concerned about the state of our cultures.

The story in the book of Daniel gives us insight into what Satan is seeking to do on a cosmic level. Daniel tells of a prayer he offered eagerly for 21 days without receiving a response. This was unusual, for Daniel's prayers were typically answered quickly and decisively. Here is Daniel's recounting of what happened:

In the third year of Cyrus king of Persia, a revelation was given to Daniel. . . . Its message was true and it concerned a great war. The understanding of the message came to him in a vision.

91

At that time I, Daniel, mourned for three weeks. I ate no choice food; no meat or wine touched my lips; and I used no lotions at all until the three weeks were over. On the twenty-fourth day of the first month, as I was standing on the bank of the great river, the Tigris, I looked up and there before me was a man dressed in linen, with a belt of the finest gold around his waist. His body was like chrysolite, his face like lightning, his eyes like flaming torches, his arms and legs like the gleam of burnished bronze, and his voice like the sound of a multitude.

I, Daniel, was the only one who saw the vision; the men with me did not see it, but such terror overwhelmed them that they fled and hid themselves. So I was left alone, gazing at this great vision; I had no strength left, my face turned deathly pale and I was helpless. Then I heard him speaking, and as I listened to him, I fell into a deep sleep, my face to the ground.

A hand touched me and set me trembling on my hands and knees. He said, "Daniel, you who are highly esteemed, consider carefully the words I am about to speak to you, and stand up, for I have now been sent to you." And when he said this to me, I stood up trembling.

Then he continued, "Do not be afraid, Daniel. Since the first day that you set your mind to gain understanding and to humble yourself before your God, your words were heard, and I have come in response to them. But the prince of the Persian kingdom resisted me twenty-one days. Then Michael, one of the chief princes, came to help me, because I was detained there with the king of Persia. Now I have come to explain to you what will happen to your people in the future, for the vision concerns a time yet to come."

Daniel 10:1–14

What is significant for us in this story is, first of all, Daniel's description of the messenger. It is clear that the messenger is an angel. It is also clear that he is a powerful angel. But there is a more powerful angel, designated the "prince of the Persian kingdom," who was able to resist him and keep him from carrying God's answer to Daniel. Then we are introduced to Michael, "one of the chief princes," clearly here an even more powerful angel than the prince of the Persian kingdom. Michael forced the prince of the Persian kingdom back, and the first angel was released to carry God's message to Daniel.

This incident in Daniel's life gives us insight into one of the least understood strategies of Satan. Satan not only sends evil spirits to demonize individuals but also assigns powerful angels to influence the course of nations and peoples. These "princes" try to affect the course of national history and to corrupt the culture of nations and peoples, twisting what is good and beneficial into what is harmful and evil.

Satan on Earth

In chapter 6 of this book we looked at the origin of demons. We discovered that demons are angels who followed Satan in a great rebellion long before the earth was created. Satan was defeated in the initial battle, and Scripture tells us repeatedly that Satan and his followers were "cast down to the earth" and had "fallen from heaven" (Isaiah 14:12; cf. Ezekiel 28:12, 16–17; Luke 10:18; Revelation 12:7–9). This repeated assertion that Satan was cast down to earth is significant. The mighty angel Lucifer, who once ranged the universe along with his many followers, is now limited to a single planet, ours.

Although Satan was defeated, he and his followers were not destroyed. They were crushed in a decisive battle that took place before Genesis 1, but they are still energized by hatred for God and a determination to do all they can to thwart His plans and purposes.

When God created Adam and Eve and shaped Eden as a place of beauty and rest in the midst of the chaos Satan had fashioned on our planet, Satan was given a new focus for his war against the Creator. It was clear God loved these creatures He had made. Satan, therefore, would concentrate his efforts on shattering the relationship between these beings and the Lord God. Even more, since God truly loved humans, Satan wanted to make human lives miserable and unproductive. God had won the major battle. But Satan would do all he could to create chaos and destroy the divine order, whether his attacks were launched against individuals through demonization or against the cultures that shaped the thoughts, the feelings, the motivations of millions.

So far in this book we have focused on Satan's attacks on individuals through demonic oppression on the outside and demonization within. In this chapter we look at Satan's broader strategy, which involves the corruption of culture and the distortion of so many good gifts God has given to human beings.

God's Good Gifts

God has a wonderful future for believers. In that future, which will be fully realized only at history's end, we human beings, transformed and fully able to love God and love each other, will be fashioned into an eternal community of love. John gives us insight into that time in Revelation 21:1–5:

> Then I saw a new heaven and a new earth, for the first heaven and the first earth had passed away, and there was no longer any

sea. I saw the Holy City, the new Jerusalem, coming down out of heaven from God, prepared as a bride beautifully dressed for her husband. And I heard a loud voice from the throne saying, "Now the dwelling of God is with men, and he will live with them. They will be his people, and God himself will be with them and be their God. He will wipe every tear from their eyes. There will be no more death or mourning or crying or pain, for the old order of things has passed away."

He who was seated on the throne said, "I am making everything new!"

A glorious future does lie ahead. But God does not intend us to live in misery now without a taste of the future blessings with which He intends to shower us. To that end, God has given us a number of wonderful gifts through which we can experience something of the coming community of love.

These gifts also serve as a focus for satanic and demonic attacks. Sometimes these attacks come through demons influencing individuals. But these attacks also come through the agency of the more powerful demons, like the prince of the Persian kingdom, who deal with the course of nations. These more powerful demons often exert their influence by corrupting a nation's culture, and thus directly attacking the gifts that God has given us.

I have devoted an entire book to the study of how Satan and his demon princes seek to overcome with evil all the good in the gifts God has given us, and how we as individuals can overcome the corruption in our own lives and families. I name below thirteen good gifts and in the next section focus on two of them. If you want to pursue this aspect of biblical demonology regarding Satan's strategies and our responses, I invite you to read *Satan Exposed: Defeating the Powers of Darkness* (Chosen, 2015).

What, then, are some of the gifts that God has provided through which we can potentially experience some of the blessings of the coming eternal Kingdom of love?

There is the gift of the *core community*, intimate relationship between husband and wife. There is the gift of *family*, intended to be a safe haven within which children can grow and mature. There is the gift of *a community of faith*, where individuals can come to know and love one another and encourage each other in a closer walk with Jesus. There is the gift of *restoration* following our sins and failures. There are good gifts of *choice, Law, God's discipline, uniqueness, provision, truth, peace, unconditional acceptance* and *eternal life—now*.

Each of these and many other gifts are "good." In the root meanings found in the Hebrew Old Testament and in the Greek New Testament, the good is always right, beneficial and beautiful.

Satan's goal is to corrupt God's good gifts with evil. And the root meaning of *evil* is, first and foremost, "wicked and harmful actions that result in pain and misery."

There is little we can do to change the course of our culture. But Paul tells us in Romans 12:21 not to be "overcome by evil, but overcome evil with good." However successful Satan might be in corrupting culture, we have the opportunity to live our lives by God's Word, to commit to doing good and to experience something out of that community of love that God intends His people to know fully at history's end.

Let's look more closely at two of God's good gifts, Satan's strategy in them and our response.

The Gift of Family

God intends the family to be a safe place, the context in which children can grow and mature into godly adults. My own research has shown that eighth-graders who felt close to God and knew that God was real reported in every case that they believed God was real to their parents. For children to experience something of God's love, those who care for them must experience God's love themselves. A second essential element in a truly nurturing family is expressed in Deuteronomy 11:18: "Fix these words of mine in your hearts and minds." Adults are to grasp God's priorities and values and to live the truth as we understand it. A third essential is to share God's Word in an informal, rather than formal schooling, context. It is in the process of sharing life that hearts and minds are shaped.

One of Satan's most vicious attacks on culture is his attack on the family. In 1960 just 5 percent of all births in the United States were to unmarried women. In 2011, that number had risen to 41 percent. In 1960, 37 percent of all American households included a married couple raising their children. Today this pattern includes just 16 percent of households. Children need stable, safe and loving homes with two parents who are committed to each other and to their children.

There is little we can do to change this cultural trend away from the nuclear family. The millennial generation especially views experimental "living together" as perhaps more valid than traditional marriage. But in spite of the culture around them, families can strive to function as a safe and loving context in which children can grow to adulthood. For this to happen, there simply must be significant interaction between children and adults. A basic strategy of Satan, then, is to find ways to limit or eliminate this kind of interaction.

The first of Satan's tactics to accomplish this is to isolate children by age group. Children typically are so grouped for most activities; school, sports, even Sunday school and church. The result is that the only significant relationship children and youth have are with children of the same age. The pervasiveness of age grading limits any significant contact children might have with adults or older children who could serve as role models. Yet it is in day-to-day settings that faith is both taught and caught. Children need relationships with adults and young people who know and love the Lord.

The second tactic Satan uses is to so fill the lives of parents that they have little quality time to spare for the boys and girls. It is understandable in today's economy that most adults must work, perform household chores, find time for each other and rest. Yet a recent study indicates that in the United States fathers spend only about ten minutes a day with their children! It is ironic that other studies reveal that adults in our society spend at least four hours a day sitting in front of the television.

The third tactic of Satan is to encourage the use of media as a substitute for interpersonal relationships. Even young children have computers and cell phones and are adept at texting, Facebook and Twitter. Most of the younger generation collect "friends" easily online but have few true friends they interact with regularly. This is deadly in terms of building relationships and learning how to communicate well with others. And it is deadly in terms of informal communication of faith.

Deuteronomy 6 and 11 picture close families. Parents love God and live by His Word. And they share much of their lives with their children, including explaining the choices they make by relating them to principles of God's Word. If we are to enjoy the good God intended for families, we need to understand Satan's tactics and how to counter them.

Here are just a few suggestions to help you counter Satan's attacks on your family. Give children unconditional love and acceptance. Spend time with children, sharing activities appropriate to their ages. Spend time with each child individually. Involve children in family discussions and decisions. Consider participating in homeschooling. Read aloud to children and talk about questions that emerge. Limit the number of organized, age-graded sports the children participate in. Encourage neighborhood playgroups. Limit and supervise the use of computers, cell phones, etc. Develop family traditions: places we vacation, things we do. As the children grow older, encourage participation with adults in various activities. Find a family service project in which all can participate. Explain your family's plan for giving, and encourage children to participate.

These are just a few of the many ways that we can help our families become more of that community of love that God intends for all.

The Gift of Uniqueness

If you have ever heard a young girl complain almost desperately that she is fat, even though the mirror and her parents tell her how slim and pretty she really is, you can understand why many in our society do not appreciate their own uniqueness. Yet in Psalm 139:13 David praises God as the one who "created my inmost being." God shaped David to be just the person he became, and God is personally involved in shaping us into the unique individuals we become. This view might be readily accepted by the successful professional athlete or the Rhodes scholar. Too many of us, however, hover around average: plain girls living in a society that worships beauty; those who are not gifted struggling to make a living. To such the idea that God shaped us personally and celebrates our uniqueness may seem ironic.

Satan is ready and eager to take advantage of our differences and to blind us to the value that we each have as distinct individuals. Satan uses differences to promote hostility; he seeks to make us dissatisfied and attacks our sense of self-worth; he stimulates covetousness and strife. If we are to overcome the evil Satan intends regarding God's gift of uniqueness, we need to understand some things that God values about each and every one of us.

The apostle Paul tells us in 1 Corinthians 12 that the Christian community, the Body, "is a unit, though it is made up of many parts" (verse 12). He points out that each part of the Body has its own function. And then Paul makes this amazing statement: "In fact God has arranged the parts in the body, every one of them, just as he wanted them to be" (verse 18). And there is more: God has given us the spiritual gifts that we need to function in our roles within the Body. The text says: "To each one the manifestation of the Spirit is given for the common good" (verse 7), and this is "just as he determines" (verse 11). Paul even says that "those parts of the body that seem to be weaker are indispensable, and the parts that we think are less honorable we treat with special honor." Not only is each one of us unique, but each one of us in our uniqueness is an indispensable part of the Body of Christ.

Satan uses our uniqueness to create jealousy and envy in order to undermine unity in the Body of Christ and to keep each of us from understanding just how important we are in God's overall plan and purpose.

How do we overcome the evil that Satan intends in distorting and disguising the significance of uniqueness?

We repudiate the idea of superiority. We are not called to feel superior because of our individual talents, the denomination we belong to or the doctrines we affirm. God has called us to know Jesus, to love others, to serve them. These things are simple enough to understand. They are beyond no one, even an individual like my daughter, Joy, who was brain damaged at birth. Today Joy lives in a family-like community with another disabled adult named Becky and a caretaker who is a retired social worker. Joy loves

God, loves to sing hymns, loves to help her friend Becky in little ways and is a truly caring person. I would not have asked God to allow the brain damage that set Joy's course in life at birth. But I do praise God that in her uniqueness she is loving Him and others as well as she can.

We honor one another. The apostle Paul picks up this theme in Philippians 2:3: "Do nothing out of selfish ambition or vain conceit [that is, refuse the notion of superiority], but in humility consider others better than yourselves." In the Greek *better than* emphasizes significance rather than superiority. When we see others as truly significant, no matter who they are or what their talents are, we will live with them as the next verse in Philippians directs: "Each of you should look not only to your own interests, but also to the interests of others." By honoring one another we combat the evil that Satan intends to introduce through our uniqueness, and we overcome that evil with good.

We commit to servanthood. We are unique, and we should celebrate the uniqueness of those around us. In Philippians 2, Paul moves to the description of how Christ humbled Himself. Jesus left His position in heaven to become a human being and to undergo an agonizing death on the cross. Paul says, "Your attitude should be the same as that of Christ Jesus" (Philippians 2:5). We are not to use our uniqueness to lord it over others but rather to serve them. As Christ told His followers, "Whoever wants to become great among you must be your servant, and whoever wants to be first must be your slave—just as the Son of Man did not come to be served, but to serve, and to give his life as a ransom for many" (Matthew 20:26–28).

When we repudiate the idea that we are in some way superior to others, when we honor each other's uniqueness and when we commit to using our uniqueness in service to others, we overcome

Satan's efforts to use our uniqueness for evil. We overcome evil with good.

TO TALK ABOUT

1. Why do you suppose spiritual warfare books focus on demonic attacks on individuals and tend to overlook Satan's grander strategies?

2. Which of the thirteen "good gifts" named in this chapter do you see Satan attacking in our culture? In your own life?

3. What do you think his tactics might be in carrying out the strategy you chose in answering #2 above? How might you as an individual overcome Satan's attempts to do evil by doing good?

10

Meet the Savior

It is strange. As we have looked through this book, we have discovered more and more about demons and quite a bit about angels. We have delved into their origins, we have looked at the rebellion of those who chose to repudiate relationship with the Creator and follow an envious and resentful angel named Lucifer, who was intent on replacing the Creator as the most powerful being in the universe. We have looked at a great battle where Lucifer, now called Satan or the devil, and his followers were decisively defeated and thrown onto an earth, which was then a jumbled, ruined battleground. We are not told how long this condition lasted. We are not told of any events or developments that took place during what must have been a vastly extended period of time. We can only sense the frustration and fury of Satan and his followers as they were forced to live on a tiny planet in a vast universe shining brightly with a million billion galaxies. It likely seemed as if any hope of victory through direct confrontation was past. Then the Creator introduced something totally new, the first indication that He has a plan for the future that involves a final judgment for Satan, the evil spirits who are his followers and the eradication of evil from the universe.

If this story were science fiction, we might begin, "A long time ago in a galaxy far, far away. . . ." But the story told in the Bible is not science fiction. That story is a revelation of reality. It is an introduction to the Person we call God, a description of origins and a sketch of the future God intends for us and for His universe. As we read the Bible's story we make the amazing discovery that each one of us has a place in God's grand plan. We not only learn who God is; we also discover who we are, and who we are intended to become. Far from being science fiction, the Bible assures us that the story it tells is the simple truth.

It is a funny thing about human beings. Deep down we recognize that truth, even when we as individuals try to deny it. Every human culture, as far back as culture can be traced by archaeologists, has sensed the existence of supernatural beings who have an impact on what happens in this world. Most cultures imagine some primary god or goddess who fashioned the material world, and they typically also imagine subordinate deities with their various roles to play in human experience. Even the harshest critics of the Greek and Roman pantheons did not reject the idea of a god or several gods; rather, they rejected the beliefs commonly held about those gods when the beliefs seemed unworthy of a deity. An individual may be an agnostic or an atheist, but there are no atheistic cultures. Throughout time human beings have believed that something beyond the material was the source of the physical universe and continues to be active in it.

This, of course, is in complete harmony with what the Bible tells us. God Himself, speaking through the prophet Isaiah, affirms that "he who created the heavens, he is God; he who fashioned and made the earth, he founded it; he did not create it to be empty, but formed it to be inhabited" (Isaiah 45:18). Earlier, the prophet quotes God saying, "It is I who made the earth and created mankind upon it. My own hands stretched out the heavens; I marshaled their starry hosts" (Isaiah 45:12).

Back in Genesis 1, the story continues with a description of a refashioned earth as a home for beings who are created in the image and likeness of God. As we read those words, not only do we sense what it means to be human, but also we are given insight into the personality and character of the Creator. The once-ruined battlefield becomes a place of beauty, as God makes choices and reshapes our planet as a home for human beings. As we see God act in each of the days, we realize that He makes distinctions between good and that which is not good; that He appreciates and loves beauty; that He uses His power to give purpose to the things that He shapes; and that, above all, this home God is fashioning for humankind shows that He loves these human beings He created.

It is amazing, with such a clear revelation of God's purpose, character and love for human beings, that over untold years the vision of the true God has been replaced by so many distorted concepts. Yet even the distorted concepts—beliefs about deities each culture invents to explain what everyone knows, that behind the existence of the material universe lies a living being—reflect reality. Somehow humanity abandoned knowledge of the true God in favor of imaginary beings shaped by their imaginations.

The Bible, in telling us the story, reveals in the early chapters of Genesis what happened. Satan, unable to thwart God's purposes in direct confrontation, determined to shatter the trust that the humans had in their Creator. With the love relationship shattered, who knew what opportunities Satan and his followers might have to cause the Creator pain? We all know the story of the Fall and how Adam and Eve chose to reject allegiance to God in favor of independence.

The apostle Paul talks about this in Romans 1:18–25. This extended passage provides insight into the origin of the distorted beliefs held by human cultures and societies. In a modern analogy, it is as if God provided every human with a radio receiver and constantly sends out a clear message of just exactly who He is, but human beings do not want to hear His message. They suppress it by turning their radio volume down until it is hardly a whisper.

> The wrath of God is being revealed from heaven against all the godlessness and wickedness of men who suppress the truth by their wickedness, since what may be known about God is plain to them, because God has made it plain to them. For since the creation of the world God's invisible qualities—his eternal power and divine nature—have been clearly seen, being understood from what has been made, so that men are without excuse.
>
> For although they knew God, they neither glorified him as God nor gave thanks to him, but their thinking became futile and their foolish hearts were darkened. Although they claimed to be wise, they became fools and exchanged the glory of the immortal God for images made to look like mortal man and birds and animals and reptiles.
>
> Therefore God gave them over in the sinful desires of their hearts to sexual impurity for the degrading of their bodies with one another. They exchanged the truth of God for a lie, and worshiped and served created things rather than the Creator—who is forever praised.

Paul's description of what happened gives us insight into the reason for the corrupted beliefs about God, and also into the moral impact of failing to respond to God's revelation of Himself. This is where the first part of the Bible story seems to end. Human beings have chosen against maintaining a relationship with the God who created them, and in the process have lost knowledge of who He truly is. Humankind is pictured as now wandering in a confusing universe and, their relationship with God broken, vulnerable to sinful passions and divine judgment. But when the Creator steps into the Garden where Satan has just succeeded in getting Adam and Eve to repudiate their relationship with God, He comes to announce judgment on Satan and to warn Adam and Eve of the impact of their choice on the entire human race.

The question the story poses is this: Can we ever recover not just the knowledge of God but an intimate personal relationship with Him, in which our tendency to harm ourselves and others by sinful choices is broken, and we again experience the love that God has always had for us?

At this point the story develops rapidly, even though the next stage takes place over millennia. The proud intent of humankind to live independently of God leads to cultures and societies where "every inclination of the thoughts of his heart was only evil all the time" (Genesis 6:5). God sent a great flood that only one family survived. Yet as time passed, humankind returned to the same ways, and the majority fell victim to the same corrupt beliefs and morals that had marked mankind since the first couple's disastrous choice of independence. During this era Satan and his demons promoted both the false religions and the moral corruption of the people in an effort to cause pain to the Creator.

Despite the darkness that ruled for thousands of years, God was quietly active. He chose a family, that of Abraham, and promised that He would bless all people through this man and his seed (see Genesis 12:1–3). As the centuries passed, God remained committed to Abraham's descendants, known in the Bible as Israel. He shaped history carefully to bring about the conditions that were right for the appearance of the promised deliverer who would put down sin and Satan once and for all. A deliverer who would restore the personal relationship between God Himself and humans that He intended in fashioning us in His own image and likeness.

As these years of darkness continued, flashes of light could be seen through the clouds: Scripture introduces prediction upon prediction about the coming Savior and His mission. And then the promised Child is born to a couple named Joseph and Mary.

Some seven hundred years before the birth of this baby, whom His parents called Jesus, the prophet Isaiah wrote puzzling words about Him:

> Who has believed our message and to whom has the arm of the LORD been revealed? He grew up before him like a tender shoot, and like a root out of dry ground. He had no beauty or majesty to attract us to him, nothing in his appearance that we should desire him.
>
> Isaiah 53:1–2

He seemed to be an ordinary baby, as if any baby seemed "ordinary" to doting parents. When this child was lovingly laid in a manger in a cattle barn, He looked no different from the thousands and millions of babies that had been born since Adam and Eve had their first child. Even as Jesus grew up in the tiny town of Nazareth, in the district of Galilee, He seemed totally ordinary. The Bible does not focus on His childhood, but we can imagine Him playing with neighborhood children and at an early age being apprenticed to His father, Joseph, who was a builder.

Later, after Jesus began to travel and make a name for Himself, one of His neighbors dismissed Him, saying, "Isn't this the carpenter's son?" In the idiom of the day, to be the son of a carpenter meant to be a carpenter oneself, so we know that as Jesus moved into adulthood He worked as a builder, a day laborer who lived near the far side of the poverty line. Certainly the prophet Isaiah was right to say that "he had no beauty or majesty to attract us to him." There really was "nothing in his appearance that we should desire him."

Years later, the apostle John had a different take on the birth. He opened his gospel with a stunning introduction. Yes, Jesus was born as an ordinary human being and lived the life of a first-century Jewish man, but while Jesus was an authentic human, He was also far more:

> In the beginning was the Word, and the Word was with God, and the Word was God. He was with God in the beginning. Through him all things were made; without him nothing was made that has been made. In him was life, and that life was the light of men.
>
> John 1:1–4

Yes, the seemingly ordinary young Jewish man called Jesus was also the God of the Old Testament, who existed from the beginning, who is the source of all that exists and who is the source of the life that animates human beings.

It is difficult for us to grasp the truth that one God, sharing a single essence, exists in three Persons. It was far beyond the ability of the first-century Jew, for his faith was rooted in the conviction that there was only one God rather than a concept that sounded to them like a multiplicity of gods. Yet as Jesus was introduced to the Jewish people through His teaching and miracles of healing, it was impossible to deny that this man was unique. In particular, it was difficult to dismiss the evidence of His uniqueness presented in His interactions with demons and evil spirits.

It is at this juncture that our exploration of demons and the story of Jesus seem to merge. The years during which Jesus lived on this earth saw an outburst of demonic activity. As we read the Bible there are three periods during which Satan and his followers struggled openly to block God's plans. They are, of course, always devoted to this pernicious work. But in the days of the Exodus, in the time of King Ahab and his consort, Jezebel, and here as Jesus appeared, Satan seemed to work up his followers into a frenzy of opposition.

As Jesus, now around thirty years of age, began to travel through Galilee and teach the people, evil spirits focused their attention on creating chaos in the Holy Land. Over and over Jesus found Himself called on to heal an unusually large number of sick people and to free those who had been taken captive and crippled by evil spirits. In each confrontation with evil spirits, and there are many recorded in the four gospels, Jesus cast out the demons and released their victims from the damage the evil spirits were causing.

The reactions to this demonstration of Jesus' power over the demonic were both strong and varied. The New Testament tells us that many recognized the hand of God and praised the Lord for Jesus' ministry. At the same time others, while thankful, were puzzled. Obviously Jesus was some kind of prophet sent by God, but who was He really? As for the religious leaders, Jesus, with His teachings and supernatural power to heal and to free, was a threat to their position and the respect they demanded from ordinary people. But when Jesus presented Himself as the God of the Old Testament, whom they had worshiped all their lives, it was far too much for most to accept (cf. John 8:12–59).

The prophet Isaiah continues his description of Jesus by predicting how God's own people would respond to Him: "He was despised and rejected by men, a man of sorrows, and familiar with suffering.

Like one from whom men hide their faces he was despised, and we esteemed him not" (Isaiah 53:3). The rejection was complete. Manipulated by the religious leaders, the Roman overlords who ruled the Jewish homelands condemned Jesus to death, and He was nailed to a cross, exposed to ridicule by the people God had loved so deeply.

It would seem that the Bible's story is a tragedy, filled with descriptions of the suffering of untold numbers, culminating in the suffering of the man called Jesus, who is portrayed both as an authentic human being and as God Himself, come to live a human life. But the story of Jesus is not a tragedy; it is a story of triumph.

Returning again to the prophet Isaiah, we discover that Jesus' death was the most powerful affirmation of God's love for you and me that could ever be made. Isaiah writes:

Surely he took up our infirmities and carried our sorrows, yet we considered him stricken by God, smitten by him, and afflicted. But he was pierced for our transgressions, he was crushed for our iniquities; the punishment that brought us peace was upon him, and by his wounds we are healed. We all, like sheep, have gone astray, each of us has turned to his own way; and the LORD has laid on him the iniquity of us all.

Isaiah 53:4–6

The death was more than that. It led to history's greatest miracle: the resurrection. Romans 1:3–4 introduces Jesus as God the Son as well as, in His human nature, a descendant of David. There, too, the apostle Paul provides proof that Jesus is the one His power over demons showed Him to be. Jesus "was declared with power to be the Son of God by his resurrection from the dead" (verse 4).

Through death Jesus is able to restore sinful human beings to a personal love relationship with God, taking on Himself the punishment our sins merit, a punishment that brings us peace and healing. We all truly have gone astray, demanding independence from God so that we might turn to our own way. But Jesus in His death laid the foundation for restoration of a relationship with God, personal transformation and an eternity to be lived in an endless community of love.

This is why, although the Bible story is about God's relationship with angels and demons and human beings, painted on the vast canvas of prehistory and history, the story really is about God and you and me. We see ourselves in the choice made by Adam and Eve of independence. We see our own experience reflected in the terrible consequences of that choice. As we meet Jesus in the New Testament, we realize that He and His sacrifice are the focus of the whole story, for it is only through Jesus' life, death and resurrection that God could achieve His intended purpose of enabling us to love Him completely and to experience the intensity of His love for us.

This brings us to a very personal question. How can you and I gain the benefits of all that Jesus has been willing to do for us? The Bible's answer is surprising. Continuing his introduction of Jesus in the early chapters of his gospel, John quotes Jesus' words:

> "For God so loved the world that he gave his one and only Son, that whoever believes in him shall not perish but have eternal life. For God did not send his Son into the world to condemn the world, but to save the world through him. Whoever believes in him is not condemned."
>
> John 3:16–18

It seems so simple.

I was one of the fortunate ones, born into a Christian family, surrounded by Christian community. From my earliest days I knew the outline of God's plan through the stories told me by my mother and in Sunday school. I took God and Jesus for granted, and knew somehow that the Bible's story was true.

Later when I was in the Navy, I began to doubt. I did not doubt the story, but somehow it did not seem that I was a part of the Bible's story. Then I learned that those words *whoever believes in Him* have a deeper meaning that I had not understood. I came to realize that *believe* means more than "to agree that what the Bible says is trustworthy." I came to realize that to *believe* called for me to make a personal commitment to this Jesus on whom the whole Bible focuses. I needed to rely completely on Jesus, not only for the forgiveness of sins but also for everything else in my life. To believe in Jesus meant that I was to commit myself totally to Him, to love Him and serve Him as best I could, and to be willing to do anything He wanted me to do.

So it was in the United States Navy in 1951 that I sat in my office upstairs at 58th and 1st Avenue in Brooklyn, New York, and told God that, while I thought I had believed in Him all my life, if I had not made the commitment to rely on Him completely, I did then.

From that day, some 66 years ago, I have never doubted God's love for or commitment to me. I have often fallen short, as every human being does. But I have experienced the joy of knowing that I have been forgiven for Jesus' sake and that I am a child of God, looking forward to an eternity with my Savior and millions of brothers and sisters who also have placed their faith and trust in Jesus.

As I write this, I do not know how you fit into God's story. The chances are, if you are reading this book, you assume that what the Bible tells us—about demons, the Creation and Jesus—is true. My prayer is that belief in Jesus might grow daily into total reliance on Him as your Lord and Savior. That if you have never made that initial commitment of faith, you will do it now. And that you will find the assurance of forgiveness and of the unconditional love of the God who sent His Son to die for you.

TO TALK ABOUT

1. How do you suppose that observing Jesus' interaction with demons changed the perspective of His contemporaries on who He might be?

2. How does observing Jesus' interaction with demons affect your perspective on who He might be?

3. If you are a person who has always believed what the Bible says about Jesus, have you passed the point of simply believing it to relying on Jesus Christ personally as Savior and Lord? If not, why wait to take this true step of faith?

Part 2

A DELIVERANCE
DICTIONARY

Introduction

It may seem strange that we need a special dictionary for words associated with deliverance and deliverance ministry. But often we do. Take, for instance, two very common words: *up* and *down*. We all attribute the same meanings to these words. Unless, of course, we are physicists talking about "up" particles and "down" particles. Then *up* and *down* have specialized and very different meanings from what they mean in ordinary speech.

Actually, many words take on different shades of meaning according to the way in which they are used. This does not mean that a word's meaning is totally changed, as in the case of *up* and *down* in physics. But words can have different implications in different contexts.

Take astrology, for example. We know that it is a study of the heavens with a view to guiding human choices. According to an ancient astrological text written on papyrus, concerning the influence of the moon at various stages of its orbit, when the moon is in Capricorn, "say whatever you wish for best results." Here we have entered the realm of ancient magick; actually the realm of demonology. The ancients (and some modern neopagans) were convinced that magick could be used with great success by manipulating and invoking the assistance of astral spirits when the stars were in appropriate alignment. And suddenly we find ourselves in a realm that is intimately linked with deliverance. Astrology becomes a tool not simply for making life decisions; it becomes a tool for tapping into the power of astral spirits who will carry out the demands of the conjurer.

That is why a deliverance dictionary is such an important element in a book like this. If you read books on deliverance or are talking with a New Age individual who uses terms that you are not familiar with, such as *spirit guide,* it is helpful not only to understand the common meaning of the words but also to understand what these words mean when used in the context of demonology and deliverance.

So in this section of this book, we launch into a discussion of some words that might seem familiar but that carry different shades of meaning or have special implications when used in the context of deliverance and demonology.

May this section and its discussions prove helpful to you.

Larry Richards

Abuse

Abuse can be verbal, physical or sexual in nature. Any type of abuse is widely viewed in deliverance ministry to make a person vulnerable to demonization. Abuse stimulates intense emotions, which are viewed as open doors through which evil spirits may enter a person's life. Thus, the problem is not so much the abuse itself but the powerful and very natural emotions the abuse stimulates, such as fear, anger, hatred, self-loathing and shame.

Many in deliverance ministry use questionnaires to help identify any abuse the person seeking deliverance has experienced, with childhood abuse viewed as especially important. While most counselors will set aside time to encourage the individual to talk about life experiences, those in this ministry will attempt to determine if any demonization has its roots in some sort of abuse.

If one or more instances of abuse are identified, many deliverance ministers will seek to deal with underlying emotional damage before commanding the demon or demons to leave. This is done, in part, because the individual needs to experience inner healing that will bless him or her. It is also done, in part, because the demon(s) usually claim they have a "legal right" to be there based on the individual's response to the abuse. Dealing with the emotional damage removes this so-called legal right to the victim's life.

This inner healing process sometimes involves asking the individual seeking deliverance to close his or her eyes and think back to the time(s) the abuse took place. The deliverance minister will often encourage the individual to try to picture where Jesus is and what He is doing. Many respond by picturing Jesus present while the abuse is taking place, often with tears in His eyes or reaching out to comfort the victim. The individual is often asked to share how it feels to know that Jesus was present and cared so deeply about the victim's suffering.

The deliverance minister will often follow up this visualization by inviting the individual to forgive the abuser and, if the person has felt anger against God for permitting the abuse, to "forgive" God, too. We cannot blame God for permitting painful experiences that are always in some way linked back to our own or others' sins. The visualization process described above will not only modify the original reactions to the abuse but also release any bitterness or anger directed against the Lord.

When inner healing is successful and the individual has forgiven all involved in the original abuse, most deliverance ministers believe that any legal ground an evil spirit claims for being present in the person's life has been removed and that the evil spirit's grip on the person has been weakened. It is ideally at this point that the demon or demons involved are commanded to leave the victim—now victor—and never to return.

See *Legal Right*.

Addiction

Among the many definitions of *addiction* found in dictionaries and other sources, probably the simplest and most inclusive are the best, for example: *Addiction* is basically "a strong and harmful need to have something regularly (such as a drug or alcohol) or to do something regularly (such as gamble or look at pornography)."

Deliverance ministers generally view *addiction* as "any compulsion that an individual has tried to break but finds impossible to control." The category of additions includes all the typical things, such as addiction to alcohol, drugs or sex. But it also includes other compulsions that gain control over a person, such as addiction to shopping, food or even watching TV. Most individuals, when they realize that they have a harmful addiction and want to be free from it, will try willpower, counseling or recovery programs such as the Twelve-Step program offered by Alcoholics Anonymous. In many cases such approaches are successful. But when a person has desperately tried everything to break a compulsion, deliverance ministers see a good chance that demonic oppression is involved.

In this situation the normal approach to deliverance will typically be followed: Identify, if possible, the source of the addiction; name the demon or demons involved; and, in the name of Jesus, cast out the demon, freeing the individual from the compulsion. It is always important in such cases to link the freed individual to a person or group who will provide both support and accountability, as there will almost always be an effort by the demons involved to recapture the individual who has been freed from an addiction.

Alter

The term *alter* is an abbreviation drawn from the phrase *alter ego,* literally meaning "another self." Only in the last few decades has the existence of alters been widely accepted as evidence of a true psychological disorder, the Dissociative Identity Disorder (DID).

Included among criteria for a diagnosis of DID, the *Diagnostic and Statistical Manual of Mental Disorders*, 5th ed., stipulates the presence of "two or more distinct identities or personality states," as well as "gaps in the recall of everyday events, important personal information and/or traumatic events." In addition, the dissociative individual has "trouble functioning in one or more major life areas because of the disorder."

One of these identities is known as the "host" or "dominant" identity and others are known as "alters" or "parts." The most widely publicized clinical case is that of Sybil Isabel Dorsett, who had developed sixteen different distinct personalities—of which she was unaware. The current psychodynamic perspective views DID as a developmental disorder that emerges due to severe and prolonged abuse or trauma, often sexual in nature, occurring in early childhood. Studies have shown that this dissociation or "splitting" typically serves as a coping mechanism to protect the individual from overwhelming emotions or situations. The dominant personality and other personalities may or may not be aware of one another. Many see the goal for treatment of DID as gradually and with sensitivity encouraging the merging of any alters with the dominant identity.

Deliverance ministers have been slow to recognize the reality of DID. Often when one of the alters emerges and takes control of an individual the phenomenon is confused with demonization. Deliverance ministers will profit from the book *Dissociative Identity Disorder* (Restoration in Christ Ministries, 2009) by a Christian couple, Tom R. and Diane W. Hawkins, who developed a distinctive ministry to help recognize and restore survivors of traumatic abuse.

The issue has been complicated not only by confusing DID with demonization, but also by the fact that alters themselves may be demonized apart from any demonization of the dominant personality. An especially helpful section of the Hawkins' book is the section on diagnostic tools and clues for recognizing DID in adults and in children.

While DID is not a common phenomenon, anyone in or contemplating a deliverance ministry needs to be aware of the way that it can be misunderstood as demonization, and of the fact that even when diagnosed correctly as dissociation, one or more of the alters may themselves be demonized. Much discernment and prayer is required when dealing with a person who has alters.

Ancestral Actions

See *Curses*, *Generational Curses* and *Sins of the Fathers*.

Anger

The Old and New Testaments each have much to say about anger and the fact that it may be expressed righteously or sinfully.

The Hebrew words used in the Old Testament text depict anger as a physical and emotional reaction, felt as a hot rush of fury. Anger is relational; it emerges when someone says or does something that violates a relationship. Moses, for example, was righteously angry with the people of Israel at Sinai when they shaped the golden calf to worship (see Exodus 32:19). But there are dangers. In Psalm 4:4, we are warned: "In your anger do not sin."

The New Testament expands upon this potential. Unchecked, anger is the root of the kind of bitterness that moves humans to murder. James advises, "Everyone should be quick to listen, slow to speak and slow to become angry, for man's anger does not bring about the righteous life that God desires" (James 1:19–20). Significantly, anger is the only powerful negative emotion that Scripture links directly to Satan. In Ephesians 4:26–27, Paul quotes Psalm 4:4 and then warns: "Do not let the sun go down while you are still angry, and do not give the devil a foothold."

David in Psalm 37 describes a perspective that enables us to avoid sinful reactions when we become angry: "Be still before the LORD and wait patiently for him; do not fret when men succeed in their ways, when they carry out their wicked schemes" (verse 7). We are to trust God to deal with the violations that stimulate our anger, and not focus on them—"fret"—when the violators seem to be successful in what David describes as their "wicked schemes." When we become angry, that emotion warns us to examine and to deal with ourselves, rather than serving as justification for striking back. And a godly response to anger provides significant protection from demonization.

Those in deliverance ministry typically view fierce anger in their clients' lives from one of three major perspectives. First, anger is viewed as an open door to a demonic presence. Most in deliverance ministry feel that holding on to anger and the bitterness anger breeds will be sensed by demons and serve as an invitation to enter a human's personality; the strong negative emotion harmonizes with the nature of demons. Also, demons of anger tend to claim that their victim's anger itself has provided a legal basis for their presence in a person's life.

A second view of anger in deliverance ministry is its use as a diagnostic aid. While it is normal for us to feel angry when we have been violated in some way, the intensity and persistence of anger, and its escalation into fits of rage during which a person seems to lose control, may very well indicate demonization. As is the case with most indicators of demonization, it is important to deal with the emotional damage that lies at the root of the anger. For this the deliverance minister may want to turn to inner healing or something similar to guide the individual to confess and repent of the response of anger and to express forgiveness of the one who violated the relationship. At this the deliverance minister will call out and expel any demons of anger, hatred, bitterness or rage present.

Third, deliverance ministers also appropriately use the word *anger* as a proper noun and will address the demon who is present and exacerbating the individual's emotion as "demon Anger." This is because demons go by functional names; that is, they take their names from the effects that they stimulate in or intensify in an individual.

It is important in deliverance ministry to identify and name the demon who is acting out both in and through his victim. As we have seen from Scripture, anger is a common and "normal" response, which may or may not be justified. At the same time, it is our responsibility to deal with our own anger and not let anger move us to sin. When extreme anger is recognized as a symptom of demonization, the demon responsible does need to be identified and addressed by name. No demon will want to be named, for when addressed by name and commanded in the name of Jesus to release and leave a victim, the demon must go.

Anointing

The concept of anointing has deep roots in the Old and New Testaments. The Hebrew word, found 69 times in the Old Testament, means "to apply oil." It is linked ritually to setting aside an object or person to the service of God. In addition to its ritual uses, anointing was used to induct leaders, such as priests, kings and, at times, prophets into their offices.

The New Testament has three different words translated "anoint." Each has the same basic meaning of spreading oil or ointment. One of these words is always used figuratively, in the sense of some special commission given by God for which a person is set apart. A second is literal, referring to the act of rubbing oil or ointment on the body. The third word is found only in 1 John 2:20, 27. This word focuses our attention on that with which one has been anointed, and the passage is universally understood to refer to the Holy Spirit.

When used in the context of deliverance ministry, *anoint* and *anointing* may have one of several meanings. These meanings generally reflect a charismatic orientation to pneumatology. Within this framework, anointing may refer to (1) the baptism with the Holy Spirit; (2) special empowerment that the anointing provides; (3) or the coming of the Holy Spirit on a demonized individual, frequently responded to by unusual manifestations.

Those in the traditional evangelical church do not regard some of the biblical terminology in the same way as charismatics. Charismatics, for instance, tend to view the "baptism with the Holy Spirit" as a "second work of grace" that comes upon a believer by the Holy Spirit for empowerment, subsequent to his or her salvation and initial indwelling. Traditional evangelicals tend to view salvation and the gift of the Holy Spirit as taking place immediately when an individual believes in Jesus, with no subsequent experience.

Ignoring who is right and who is wrong in a theological dispute, we must say that the charismatic community has continually maintained a clearer focus on the significance of the work of the Holy Spirit in believers' lives and in deliverance ministry. A deep and abiding understanding that even Jesus cast out demons in the power of the

Spirit reminds us that we, too, must rely completely on God's Spirit as we seek to release others from their bondage to demonization.

Apostle

By the first century, the word *apostle* was used to identify a personal representative of the one sending him. In the gospels twelve individuals are identified as *the* apostles of Jesus. Later Paul is recognized as equal to the original Twelve. In Scripture, however, a number of other people are identified as apostles (cf. Acts 14:14; Romans 16:7). There is no indication in the New Testament of an office of apostle or of an institutional apostolic role in a local congregation. It seems likely that the closest parallel in historic and modern Christianity to the role of apostle is that of missionary, as both are chosen by God and sent forth to spread the message of His Son throughout the world.

At times some deliverance ministers claim the title *apostle*. It is important for us to remember that in using the title no one is claiming the authority of the original Twelve or of the apostle Paul. Rather, that individual is emphasizing the privilege of representing Jesus to the unsaved and serving as His agent to bring deliverance to those who are held captive by Satan and his demons.

Astrology

The practice of astrology is rooted in the idea that the physical proximities of heavenly bodies have a controlling influence on what happens on earth. In the ancient world astrology was one of the occult sources through which individuals sought guidance for their lives and decisions. It, like other occult practices, is condemned in Deuteronomy 18:9–13. The prophet Isaiah ridicules those who rely on such occult sources for guidance.

> "Keep on, then, with your magic spells and with your many sorceries, which you have labored at since childhood. Perhaps you will succeed, perhaps you will cause terror. All the counsel you have received has only worn you out! Let your astrologers come forward, those stargazers who make predictions month by month, let them save you from what is coming upon you. Surely they are like stubble; the fire will burn them up. They cannot even save themselves from the power of the flame."
>
> Isaiah 47:12–14

While many think that consulting an astrologer or casually checking out predictions in the daily newspaper is a harmless practice, Scripture takes astrology and all other occult practices seriously. Any such practice may bring an individual into contact with the supernatural realm and the demons who inhabit it. This is why those in deliverance ministry are careful to lead a person to repudiate astrology and similar dabbling in the occult. Decisively rejecting such practices is an essential element of remaining free from demonization.

Authority

The basic concept expressed in the biblical words most often translated "authority" is "freedom of action." The person with authority is free to act in ways that a person without authority, or under authority, is not. God is and has the ultimate freedom of action: a freedom to act that cannot be limited by anyone or anything. When a person in deliverance ministry speaks of "authority" he or she generally claims the specific freedom to order demons to leave an individual they have been oppressing. This basis for claim is firmly rooted in Scripture.

While Jesus was on earth the crowds were overwhelmed by His exercise of authority. He spoke with authority, unlike the religious leaders who quoted one another endlessly to validate their inter-pretations. He claimed the authority to forgive sin—an authority reserved for God alone—and then demonstrated His authority by a miraculous healing. And Jesus claimed and demonstrated His authority over the spirit world by casting out many demons.

The gospels make it clear that Christ then delegated authority over evil spirits to His disciples. Matthew 10:1 states, "He called his twelve disciples to him and gave them authority to drive out evil spirits." Later in His ministry Jesus selected 72 "others" of His followers, who had no claim to being apostles, and "sent them two by two ahead of him to every town and place where he was about to go" (Luke 10:1). Luke then tells us that "the seventy-two returned with joy and said, 'Lord, even the demons submit to us in your name'" (Luke 10:17). Clearly, Jesus' authority over demons had been delegated to these followers of His who had no official position in the community of faith.

Acts contains reports of the exercise of this authority by Paul and others, and the writings of the early Church fathers portray the casting out of demons by laypersons as a common occurrence. As the church became more hierarchical, deliverance was gradually limited to a priest appointed by a bishop, who used an established ritual to perform exorcisms.

Today a number of both Catholic and Protestant laypersons as well as ministers claim the authority that they believe Jesus gives to all Christians to expel demons in Jesus' name. In our day, in some branches of the Church, the authority Jesus gives to believers over demons is being rediscovered and exercised.

Baptism with the Spirit

Also baptism "of," "in" or "by" the Spirit. The work of the Holy Spirit in believers is a major theme in the epistles. At the same time that work is complex and the subject of many analogies. Christians are to walk in the Spirit, to live by the Spirit and to avoid grieving the Holy Spirit. It is not surprising with so many varied references to the Holy Spirit's work in believers that there should be different understandings of just what baptism with the Spirit is, and how this affects the practice of deliverance ministry. The interpretation and use of the phrase in deliverance ministry depends on the theological frame of reference of the writer or practitioner. There are essentially two basic frames of reference from which deliverance ministers operate: the charismatic frame of reference and what I call the traditional evangelical frame of reference.

The charismatic frame of reference is rooted in descriptions of events that took place in the church of Acts. In the gospels John the Baptist introduced water baptism as an innovation that was undertaken to identify the person being baptized with Jesus Christ as Messiah and Savior. In each of the synoptic gospels John speaks of one who is about to appear, a person far more powerful than John himself, who will baptize, not with water, "but with the Holy Spirit" (Matthew 3:11; Mark 1:8; Luke 3:16). In *The New*

International Encyclopedia of Bible Words (Zondervan, 1999), I noted the following:

> The book of Acts describes the fulfillment of that promise. The baptism took place at the coming of the Spirit on Jesus's followers as reported in Acts 2 (2:1–4; cf. with Acts 10:45–47; 11:15–17). Acts describes a number of phenomena that took place at that time. The Spirit came. The Spirit filled believers. There was an outward sign of fiery tongues and a rushing wind. The Spirit empowered the believers to speak in languages other than their own.

While nothing in Acts defines specifically what baptism with the Spirit is, those in the charismatic renewal take the events described as normative. After an individual is converted, that is, born again by the Holy Spirit, then baptism with the Spirit takes place as a so-called "second work of grace." This baptism with, by or in the Spirit is normally marked by the outward sign of speaking in "tongues" (languages not one's own). And baptism with the Spirit is required to empower the believer fully to live a Christian life, to fight off demons and to minister effectively to others.

In contrast, those in the traditional evangelical camp do not question the description of what took place or doubt that Acts 2 depicts the fulfillment of Christ's promise. They do, however, question whether the events described in Acts 2 are normative or not. Simply because these events took place during the transitional period from Judaism to a fully functioning Christianity, they need not be understood as normative or a pattern to be duplicated today. Instead traditional evangelicals find in 1 Corinthians 12:13 a clear definition of baptism with the Spirit. There the text says, "We were all baptized by one Spirit into one body—whether Jews or Greeks, slave or free—and we were all given the one Spirit to drink." This text is understood by evangelicals to indicate that baptism with

A *Deliverance Dictionary*

the Spirit takes place at conversion ("we were all baptized"), and that baptism of the Spirit is an act of God by which believers are organically united to Jesus and to one another in one Body.

Rather than argue which approach to Scripture is correct, I simply note that understanding the theological frame of reference out of which any person in deliverance ministry is operating will have a significant impact on how he or she uses terms like *baptism with the Spirit* and his or her view of the role in deliverance of the spiritual gift of tongues. Anyone who reads about deliverance ministry, attends deliverance ministry seminars or is personally involved in a deliverance ministry needs to understand both the charismatic frame of reference and the evangelical frame of reference, and to be aware of the practical implications of these divergent views on one's approach to deliverance ministry and one's interpretation of what might take place in a deliverance session.

At the same time, we need to affirm the common understandings held by all in deliverance ministry. We all understand that we have no ability in and of ourselves to cast out demons, and that we cast out evil spirits in the name of and with the authority of Jesus Christ. And, for all of us, it is a joy to set Satan's prisoners free.

Binding and Loosing

The words *bind* and *loose* are found in Matthew 18:18. There Jesus promises, "I tell you the truth, whatever you bind on earth will be bound in heaven, and whatever you loose on earth will be loosed in heaven." While there is nothing in the context about demons, deliverance ministers link this verse to a passage in Matthew 12:29 where Jesus is speaking about driving demons out of a person. There

132

He says, "How can anyone enter a strong man's house and carry off his possessions unless he first ties up the strong man?" That is, to be freed to function in an area controlled by demons, one must first bind the demon and end his control. Significantly, in this broader passage Jesus is specifically speaking about demonization.

This concept of binding is frequently applied in deliverance ministry, commonly when the deliverance minister senses that a demon is blocking his attempts to minister, or is blocking the oppressed individual's ability to understand and respond to the minister's statements. In such situations deliverance ministers may, in the name of Jesus, bind the demon and forbid him to continue what he has been doing to hinder the exorcism. Loosed from this influence the process of deliverance can continue.

Black Magick

See *Magick*.

Bondage

In deliverance ministry *bondage* is a very broad term. A person may be in bondage to "ungodly beliefs" (that is, any distorted perspective that is not in harmony with Scripture). A person may be in bondage to a sinful habit or practice. A person may be in bondage to the effects of childhood sexual abuse. A person may be in bondage to a physical disability that has a spiritual or psychological cause. In short, almost anything that limits an individual's experience of his or her God-given potential might be viewed as bondage. Thus, the specific bondage of which any deliverance minister or writing refers to will be determined by the context.

The focus in deliverance ministry is to free the sufferer from any bondage that has either a demonic cause or is actively supported by demonic influence. The steps that can be taken with a given individual depend on the nature of the bondage. A person, for example, might be in bondage to bitterness and envy, intensified by a demon of bitterness. Most deliverance ministers realize that the destructive emotions of bitterness and envy need to be dealt with before or after the demon is cast out. Thus, a deliverance minister would help this person *to identify* the source, *to recognize* that however great the hurt, the person needs to acknowledge that his or her response was sinful, and *to forgive* the person or persons who caused the harm. This removes any basis for an evil spirit to claim a right to be present in the person's life, and the evil spirit can be cast out with less resistance.

We are seldom in bondage simply because of an evil spirit's presence. In most cases the roots of our bondage lie in our experiences and our responses to them, which open the door to a demonic presence and influence. As a deliverance minister helps an individual deal with the roots of his or her bondage, and then casts out any evil spirit that was using the opportunity to intensify the harm already caused, the bonds can and will be broken and the individual will find freedom in Christ.

Channeling

The occult practice of channeling, also called *trance mediumship*, is a form of spirit communication. In channeling, a spirit (identified as the "spirit communicator") links with an individual (a medium) who lends himself or herself to the spirit. In channeling, rather than give a message to the medium for him or her to repeat, the spirit is thought to communicate directly through the medium, whose consciousness is overshadowed to a greater or lesser degree. Like other occult practices, channeling through a medium is forbidden and identified as "detestable to the Lord" (Deuteronomy 18:12).

Charm

As a noun, a charm is any object used by individuals or groups to ward off evil. As a verb, to be charmed indicates that the individual has been the object of magical attempts to protect or to harm him or her. What we call charm bracelets, that have no association with the occult, are harmless. But any objects that currently or in the past have had any association with the occult are dangerous and should be destroyed.

Confession

Confession plays a significant role in deliverance ministry. The Greek word translated "confess" in the New Testament is *homologeo*. In the first-century contemporary legal system, to confess meant that the person agreed with the charge brought against him. When God calls on us in 1 John 1:9 to confess our sins, what He means is simply to agree with Him and His valuation that an action or thought was sinful. The promise associated with the challenge is this: "If we confess our sins, he is faithful and just and will forgive us our sins and purify us from all unrighteousness" (verse 9).

The emphasis here on divine forgiveness is further developed in the promise that God will "purify us from all unrighteousness." Deliverance ministry rightly places great emphasis on confession of any sins discovered in the process of an exorcism. Divine cleansing refers not only to our character but implies purification from any demonic influence.

In deliverance ministry it is important not only to be aware of any personal sins that might have opened the door to demonic influence but also to explore the impact of the sins of others and our reaction to them. Often our reaction to painful hurts and violations is anger and bitterness. This is understandable. But if we hold on to the anger and the bitterness and nurture them in our hearts, our reaction has moved into the realm of sin. Scripture says, "In your anger do not sin" (Ephesians 4:26). The surge of anger that comes when we are mistreated is understandable and very human. When we nurture this emotion and hold on to it, our reaction has moved into the realm of sin. We need to confess our sin, and experience the forgiveness and the purification that are ours in Christ.

We cannot overemphasize the importance of forgiveness in deliverance ministry. This may mean forgiving the person or persons who hurt us. It may mean "forgiving" God for permitting our experience. And it may mean forgiving ourselves for holding on to the bitterness and anger for so long. The great promise in Scripture is, first, that in Christ all our sins have been nailed to the cross. And, second, that we can experience the healing that forgiveness provides today.

Curses

Curses are a major theme in deliverance teaching. Generally a *curse* is understood as "words spoken that release negative spiritual power against an object, person or place." In the Old Testament we have many instances of God pronouncing a curse, as on Satan in Genesis 1, or as on generations of Israelites in Deuteronomy 28 should they forsake Him and violate His Law. We also have examples of individuals placing curses, as Balaam's attempt to curse Israel in Numbers 22–24. Bromiley's *International Standard Bible Encyclopedia* (Eerdmans, 1979) notes:

> When a curse is pronounced against any person we are not to understand this as a mere wish, however violent, that disaster should overtake the person in question any more than we are to understand that a corresponding "blessing" conveys simply a wish that prosperity should be the lot of the person on whom the blessing is invoked. A curse was considered to possess an inherent power of carrying itself into effect. . . . Such curses [and blessings] possess the power of self-realization.

In the *New International Encyclopedia of Bible Words* (Zondervan, 1999), I provide an analysis of words translated "curse" in the Old Testament. One Hebrew word, *'alah,* is most often used in warnings. Such curses uttered ahead of time made God's people aware of the judgments that would follow the breaking of their covenant obligations (see Deuteronomy 29:14–21). A verb found 63 times in the Old Testament, *'arar,* like *'alah,* functions as a statement of consequences embedded in the fabric of God's Law. These words go beyond defining the consequences of disobedience. They announce punishments that God has imposed. The root idea expressed in *'arar* is that "the thing or person cursed is in some way bound: that person or thing is unable to do what he, she, or it was once able to do."

To the peoples of the ancient world, and unfortunately to many in deliverance ministry, curses are viewed as magical tools used to gain power or harm enemies. With the exception of the use of the term *qabah* in the story of Balaam (Numbers 22–24), *curse* is not used in Scripture in this commonly accepted way. Biblically speaking, *curse* is a moral rather than a magical term. As far as the pagan use of magical curses, Paul tells us we are to do nothing if verbally or magically cursed that will reflect ill upon those who curse us. Paul's call is for us to "bless and do not curse" (Romans 12:14).

Curses, Then and Now

The biblical concept of curses places the curse squarely in the moral arena, where it is linked with the breakdown of relationship with God. We might call this a Type 1 curse. It is clear in the Old Testament that the habitual practice of sin, which is a violation of the covenant relationship, brings on a curse. In the New Testament, those who are accursed are under divine judgment.

The biblical story of Balaam reflects the magical, in contrast to the moral, concept of curses. In pagan cultures a curse involved enlistment of a supernatural power in an effort to harm, or to limit, someone who was viewed as a rival or enemy. We might call this a Type 2 curse. According to Fritz Graf's *Magic in the Ancient World* (Harvard University, 1999), binding spells (*defixiones*, curses) were cast by the use of rituals aided by a "demon assistant" (*parabedros*). These *defixones* were used to harm an enemy, to evoke an erotic response in a person one desired or to weaken a rival's ability. In each case the curse was intended to limit the freedom of the person cursed, thus giving the aggressor control. The effectiveness of the curse depended on its empowerment by a deity or other supernatural being. The difference between the biblical concept of curse (which is moral in nature and initiated by and enforced by God) and the pagan notion of curse (which is initiated by a human and enforced by a supernatural being) is both striking and significant.

There is a third concept of curses. This Type 3 or contemporary view of curses acknowledges that there are consequences for breaking God's Law (Type 1) and that there are supernatural attacks empowered by demons (Type 2). But, further, this view seems to focus on what are known as "word curses" and the impact of these demonically driven statements. These curses, it is believed, gain a foothold and grow in power because they are spoken by someone in rightful authority over the victim. Thus, a parent can curse a child, a pastor a congregation, etc. Further, it is generally acknowledged that word curses can continue on to affect subsequent generations as the curses travel down family or corporate lines. This idea of generational cursing from a spoken word is a new concept, but one based on an interpretation of Exodus 20:5 and Jeremiah 32:18. We will look at these passages in a moment. This view tends to dominate the thinking of those in current deliverance ministry; the breaking of word curses has a significant place in many deliverance sessions.

The Three Types: Further Understanding

In review, we have identified three ways in which *curse* is conceptualized in Scripture and contemporary deliverance ministry. It is important to identify the source of each of these concepts and the issues that each one raises.

In the biblical concept, curses are divine judgments for violations of a covenant relationship with God. The way to deal with such curses is to do away with the sins that led to their imposition. The primary question relating to such curses is whether or not they have an impact on future generations, so-called family or generational curses.

In the pagan concept, curses are supernatural attacks on a person empowered by demons. The way to break such curses is to cancel them in Jesus' name, exercising the authority Christ gives believers, and to cast out any demons present in the victim. There are no major questions linked with occult curses. Scripture and experience both make it clear that such curses have power, but cannot withstand canceling in the name of Jesus.

In the contemporary concept, curses are limits placed on someone with authority over the victim, using words empowered by demons. The way to break such curses is either withdrawal of the curse by the one who imposed it or canceling the curse in Jesus' name, exercising the authority Christ gives believers and then casting out any demons present in the victim.

While Scripture does not deal exhaustively with curses, it is clear that curses do exist, and that they are empowered by God (Type 1) or by Satan (Type 2). There are, however, no clear texts authenticating "word curses" as they are understood in the contemporary view; it has been developed predominantly from the experience of individuals in deliverance ministry. This does not mean that the contemporary view fails to portray spiritual realities accurately. It simply means that we cannot have the same level of confidence in speaking about elements of the contemporary view of cursing that we can have concerning the biblical and pagan/occult view of cursing.

At this point, let me note that experience is a valid source of data about the supernatural, just as experience is a valid source of information about the natural universe. In both spheres validity may be established based on repeated experiences independently verified by multiple observers. Everyone agrees, for instance, that water boils at 212°F at sea level. This phenomenon has been observed so often by so many with such consistent results that the belief that water boils at 212° is accepted as a fact. Applying the same principle, if we look at the many experiences of deliverance ministers who have cast demons from individuals struggling with a difficulty that has gone on generation after generation, then we can conclude that the phenomenon is very real.

I have serious doubts, however, that what we are dealing with in such cases is, in fact, the result of words spoken by someone with spiritual authority over the cursed individual. I suspect we are dealing not with curses at all, but with something very different, which, if rightly understood, would point to a significant modification in our ministry to many demonized individuals.

A Biblical Basis?

I mentioned above that, as far as many in deliverance ministry are concerned, belief in the Type 3 curse is supported by Exodus 20:5–6 and Jeremiah 32:18. These passages state:

> "I, the LORD your God, am a jealous God, punishing the children for the sin of the fathers to the third and fourth generation of those who hate me, but showing love to a thousand generations of those who love me and keep my commandments."

And:

> "You show love to thousands but bring the punishment for the fathers' sins into the laps of their children after them."

As anyone involved in deliverance ministry knows, demonization does have a generational dimension. Charles Kraft, whom I respect more than anyone in deliverance ministry, recognizes occult (ritual) cursing in his book *I Give You Authority* (Chosen, 1997), and goes on to discuss what he calls "informal cursing" by the utterance of damaging words about others or about oneself (self-cursing). His conviction is that somehow the enemy has the ability to empower such curses, in ways that may extend through generations. While Kraft points out that the sins of Christians provide a landing place for such curses, he is convinced that we are all vulnerable to the possibility of becoming victims of such word curses.

It stands without question that the foundations of an individual's oppression by demons can often be traced to parents, grandparents and even beyond. It is not surprising, then, that many in deliverance ministry look to these passages of Scripture and find an explanation for generational curses in word curses spoken by (or against) an ancestor. It seems to me, however, that there is a better explanation for the symptoms associated with what are currently viewed as generational curses.

In recent decades we have witnessed an explosion of research on the lasting impact of experiences occurring during the earliest stages of our lives. One line of research has explored the impact on the unborn child of the mother's experience during pregnancy. This research has established that stress and the associated emotions of the mother affect the child's development. Work on "attachment theory" has shown not only that a mother's style of attachment (of interacting with the child) is passed on to her infant, but that her attachment style has a dramatic and powerful impact on how the child views him or herself and relates to others as an adult. Additional research indicates that while infants orient initially to the mother, the period between age two and three is critical for a boy's orientation to his father and to the development of later control of aggression.

The point of all this research is to underline the fact that our primary caregivers, those persons with "spiritual authority" over children, have a far greater influence on us than we have imagined. It is not necessary for a parent to "speak curses" to have a dramatic negative impact on the offspring, although harmful and demeaning words have great impact on children.

This leads us back to that biblical passage that deliverance ministers rely on to explain the persistence of curses across generations. Most who quote Exodus 20 understand it to teach that God actively curses not only guilty persons but also their offspring. This is often explained by the notion that Scripture views persons within the context of the family rather than treating them, as our culture does, as individuals. This interpretation raises questions about the character of God and is contradicted by such passages as Ezekiel 18, where God states explicitly that He will consider each individual's behavior and not punish anyone for his father's sins.

How then are we to understand Exodus 20:5–6? The context is the establishment of the Ten Commandments as guidelines for maintaining healthy and loving relationships, both with God and within one's community. In this context the Law was designed to create a safe place, a sphere in which God's people could experience His blessing even though cultures around them were marred by sins that made life anything but safe. The message of these verses is that it is not safe to ignore or reject the lifestyle God lays out for His people. The person who "hates" (decisively rejects) God and His ways will introduce into the family line dynamics that will negatively impact the offspring for generations. On the other hand, the person who "loves" (chooses and adheres to God and the lifestyle He lays out) will experience positive blessings.

Viewed in context, Exodus 20:5–6 pre-announces a principle of judgment built into the very nature of human beings. Sin will create unsafe attachments, and the kinds of stress and negative emotions that emerge will necessarily distort the healthy development of infants and children, causing psychological trauma and suffering to subsequent generations.

What I suggest is that what deliverance ministers have viewed as curses empowered by demons uttered by those with spiritual authority over a victim is better understood as a result of psychological trauma caused intentionally or unintentionally by caregivers in childhood—traumas that negatively affect children's development for generations, and also cause psychic wounds to which demons can become attached.

Curse or Trauma: Does It Make a Difference?

Some might argue that whether a demonized person's situation is caused by curses or by trauma makes little difference. In either case, deliverance ministry calls for casting out the demons. I suggest that it does make a difference whether the cause is a curse or psychological trauma. Take the case of George.

George has struggled with feelings of hostility and isolation, which led to one divorce. Although he is a Christian now, his second marriage is breaking down. He is angry with God and his spouse, fearing another divorce is imminent. If we assume his problem is caused by a curse, it makes sense to break the curse and cast out the demons who empower it. It also makes sense to assume that with the curse broken, and the demons gone, George will, with a little help, go on to have a healthy marriage and repair other stressed relationships.

But now let's assume that George's struggle is rooted in psychological trauma caused by his early caregiver's failings and faulty attachment styles. It is these attachment styles that were transmitted to him and that he is now acting out in his marriage and in other relationships.

In working with George we come to the realization that demons, taking advantage of the early trauma, now have a grip on George and are exacerbating the situation. We no longer assume that George's problems are rooted in a word curse, and we realize that he needs significant help to repair the impact of his childhood trauma and to develop healthy attachment styles. The demons complicate the problem, and we will need guidance from the Holy Spirit whether to confront them and cast them out now or encourage George to get therapy first, thus weakening the grip of the demons before casting them out. Whichever approach we are led to take, we do not make the mistake of seeing the demons (or a curse) as George's underlying problem. The underlying problem is the original psychological damage, and we must deal with it either before or after ridding George of demons.

Deliverance, rightly understood, is far more than casting out demons. It is helping victims to health and wholeness—spiritually, psychologically and often physically. To the extent that our diagnosis of generational demonization focuses on word curses as a cause rather than on childhood traumas inflicted on children and repeated through the generations by those who have themselves been traumatized by fallen human parents, we are unlikely to deal with the real issues that have contributed to the demonization.

Deliverance

In its broadest sense, deliverance involves guiding Christians into the fullness of the life that Christ provided for us in His cross and resurrection. More narrowly, deliverance may be viewed as freeing believers from the influence of demonic powers. In its narrowest sense, deliverance is casting out demons in the name of Jesus.

While Christ has given believers authority over demons, there are several things that can complicate the process of deliverance. First, we must diagnose demonization. Second, we must identify the demon or demons involved. Third, it is helpful and sometimes necessary to remove any legal ground that demons claim to have in oppressing an individual. At this point, fourth, deliverance by simply casting out the demon or demons, using the authority Jesus gives us and in His name, is usually appropriate. Deliverance, however, is not necessarily complete at this point. Jesus made this clear in Matthew 12:43–45:

> "When an evil spirit comes out of a man, it goes through arid places seeking rest and does not find it. Then it says, 'I will return to the house I left.' When it arrives, it finds the house unoccupied, swept clean and put in order. Then it goes and takes with it seven other spirits more wicked than itself, and they go in and live there. And the final condition of that man is worse than the first."

It is clear from this passage that there is an essential fifth element in true deliverance: protecting the person from the return of that demon or other demons.

Diagnosing Demonization

We human beings are complex. We are physical beings with bodies that are subject to physical ills. We are also psychological beings with thoughts, emotions and volition that can be corrupted. And we are also spiritual beings with an inner sense of self and of

God, both of which can become distorted. We are spirit, soul and body. At the same time we human beings are unity. Our various aspects are not isolated from each other.

This means, for instance, that our psychological state can have an impact on our physical well-being—and vice versa: Depression and despair can be the cause as well as the consequence of physical illness. Our physical illnesses, psychological troubles and distorted ideas about God and ourselves can have totally natural causes. Yet they may correctly be identified by deliverance ministers as possible symptoms of demonization.

Demons, rather than causing our problems, typically exacerbate our natural responses; they utilize our reactions to life experiences as entry points. Anger, for instance, is a normal response to some situations. Demons do not create the anger, but they can and do intensify the anger, causing us to hold on to it and become bitter, or moving us to strike out in rage against others. This makes it difficult for us to say with certainty when deliverance from demonic influence is needed.

Typically a person looks for a deliverance minister only after seeking help from doctors or counselors. The impact of demons on the lives of individuals is generally misunderstood even by the most devout Christians. When a person does come to a minister or mature Christian friend for help, there are ways to test for demonic influence. First, we need to get a sense of the intensity of the responses that trouble the individual. Continuing with the example of anger, we might ask: How angry does the person become? Can the anger be described as uncontrollable rage? What precipitates fits of anger? Along with questions like these, we need to explore what the individual has done to try to deal with the anger. Has he or she sought help from counselors? Has he or she acknowledged the anger as sin and sought God's help in dealing with it? When any response becomes so intense that it can be described as uncontrollable, there is a good chance that demons are involved.

Identifying the Demon or Demons Involved

Demons hardly advertise their presence. Their influence is more effective when it goes unrecognized. In addition, demons are legalistic and deceptive. A demon causing a particular problem will likely not respond if addressed simply as "evil spirit" or "demon."

While Scripture reveals that at least some demons do have personal names, the names of the demons that Jesus cast out and that trouble us are functional names. That is, the name of the demon who caused an individual to be deaf and unable to speak was "Deaf and Mute" (see Mark 9:25), which is how Jesus addressed the spirit when casting him out.

This use of functional names guides us when identifying and calling out the demons we seek to deliver a person from. In the case of anger, we would address the evil spirit as "demon Anger," "demon Rage," etc. In this process we would typically command the demon in Jesus' name to reveal his presence to or through the demonized individual. That is, either the person seeking deliverance would sense the demon's presence, or the demon might speak through the demonized person.

Removing the Legal Ground

Demons gain access to an individual's life by what are typically called "entry points" or "doors." Demons will frequently claim that the way in which they entered a person's life gives them legal ground to be there. If, for example, a woman's dabbling in occult practices provided an evil spirit with an entry point into her life, the demon is likely to claim he has a right to be there because of what she did.

It is important in deliverance ministry to identify the entry point and to help the demonized individual remove that legal ground. In the case of entry through occult practice, a deliverance minister, after identifying the entry point, would guide the demonized individual to recognize and confess all association with the occult as sin. The individual would then need to repudiate every occult involvement and reject any future involvement with the occult. If there are any objects or charms associated with the occult, they should be destroyed. At this point, the evil spirit can no longer claim he has a right to be present in the individual's life and can be more easily cast out.

Exercising of Authority to Cast Out the Demon(s)

At this point it is usually appropriate to command the evil spirit in Jesus' name to leave the individual and never return.

Providing Protection Against Demonic Return

As the passage in Matthew 12 reminds us, evil spirits actively seek residence in human beings. They also know that there are certain experiences and responses that provide entry points through which demons may enter the life of an individual. These entry points range from involvement in the occult, to habitual sin, to our responses to traumas, especially those experienced early in life. An extremely important element in deliverance ministry is to identify particular entry points through which demons have gained access to the person being ministered to. If this was not done earlier in the deliverance process, it needs to be done now.

If the entry point was trauma, inner healing can help close that door to demonic reentry.

When the entry point is related to involvement in the occult, confession and repudiation, along with separating from any occult practices or objects, is essential.

When the entry point is related to habitual sins, confession and repudiation, along with abandonment of the sinful practice(s), are essential.

One aspect of providing protection against demonic return that is too often overlooked is to connect the now-delivered individual with a small group of Christians where he can be supported and encouraged in his commitment to Jesus, just as he will encourage and support other members of the group. All too often without participation in such a support group an individual will lapse, and the door(s) that initially gave evil spirits access to his life will reopen.

Deliverance does focus on casting out the demons or evil spirits who have gained influence over an individual. Yet true deliverance involves far more than telling an evil spirit in the name of Jesus to leave the person he has been oppressing. Our goal in deliverance is to free individuals from those things that hinder their relationships with Jesus and that block their experience of the abundant life that Christ came to provide.

See *Demonic Stronghold*.

Deliverance Ministry

Christian deliverance ministry refers to the cleansing of a person from demons, also known as evil spirits, in order to address problems manifesting in that individual's life. Those problems might come as a result of the presence of evil spirits or might serve as the basis of a demon's claimed right to oppress a person. Many in deliverance ministry witness physical, psychological, spiritual and emotional problems resulting from the presence of oppressing spirits. The validity of the practices and many of the underlying beliefs that shape deliverance ministries are not accepted by all Christians.

There is no indication of a specialized deliverance ministry in the early Church, although references to casting out evil spirits are common in writings of the early Church fathers. Today, too, there are churches that offer deliverance ministry to their members and to those who attend their services as just another aspect of the church's ministry. There are also a number of organizations that style themselves as deliverance ministries and offer to cast out demons, ministering to groups in seminars as well as to individuals. It is also common to find deliverance ministry emphasized as a major element of some local churches' programs. The quality and the effectiveness of deliverance ministries vary greatly; it is very important to understand the theology and the practices of any deliverance ministry before seeking help.

I recommend that anyone seeking to be involved with deliverance ministry or who feels the need of deliverance ministry contact the International Society of Deliverance Ministers (ISDM) at P.O. Box 64062, Colorado Springs, CO, 80962, or info@deliverance ministers.org. ISDM, which was founded to restore credibility to deliverance ministry, maintains a list of members that you can access and provides training in deliverance ministry at various locations in the United States.

See *Deliverance.*

Demon

Demons, also called "evil spirits," are familiar to us from their confrontations with and their defeats by Christ, as recorded in the gospels. Yet Scripture reveals far more about evil spirits than we find in the gospels.

The Old Testament refers to what we call demons by the term *elohim*, essentially meaning "spirit being" but often translated as "God" or "gods." The Lord created these spirit beings as angels long before the story of the earth's creation as told in Genesis 1. Most powerful among the angels that God created was a cherub (a title indicating the highest rank in the angelic host), who was known as "Morning Star" and "Light Bearer." He is described in Ezekiel not only as "the model of perfection" but also as "blameless in your ways from the day you were created till wickedness was found in you" (Ezekiel 28:12, 15).

Moved by a determination to supplant God as supreme ruler of the universe, this angel, who became known as Satan, led a rebellion. The result was war between God, Satan and their angelic followers. The *elohim* who followed Satan in this war—again this took place long before Genesis 1—were changed and are today known as demons or evil spirits.

Scripture gives us a few insights into the transformation of Satan's followers from angels to the demons we meet in the New Testament. We know that there was a great battle, of which Christ said: "I saw Satan fall like lightning from heaven" (Luke 10:18). This same theme is found in the Old Testament: "How you have fallen from heaven, O morning star, son of the dawn! You have been cast down to the earth" (Isaiah 14:12).

With Satan and his followers defeated, fallen from heaven and "cast down to the earth," the war was essentially over. But

God did not see fit to destroy the rebels yet. Instead he reshaped planet Earth, which Genesis 1 depicts as a war zone, "formless and empty." Then God placed a man and a woman fashioned in His image on the refashioned earth. Their mission was to overcome the evil that Satan had done and to build an eternal community of love.

When Satan realized what God had done in establishing this human beachhead in his territory, he immediately went about corrupting the first pair. To some extent Satan was successful. He did break the intimate bond of trust that existed between God and Adam and Eve. And Satan did distort the gifts that God gave humans so that they might be used for evil rather than for good. Even so, God opened the door for Adam and Eve to return to Him. Unlike Satan and his demons, humans fell but remained redeemable.

This is one of the most important things we need to remember when dealing with demons. In describing demons as "evil spirits," the New Testament uses a significant word for *evil*. This word does not, as other biblical terms do, portray evil as a flaw in an individual's character. Nor does it portray evil simply as a refusal of that which we know to be good. The word translated "evil" in the description of demons as "evil spirits" casts evil as a positive, active force. The evil spirit, like a human being, is an authentic being with a mind, emotions and freedom of choice, who takes pleasure in harming humans. Any contact a human might have with a demon or evil spirit is both dangerous and destructive.

It is vital when dealing with demons in any way to remember that they are essentially and actively evil. They have no redeeming qualities. And they take intense pleasure in defeating, tormenting and keeping believers from the full experience of the new life God has provided for us in Christ.

Demonic Oppression

In general deliverance ministers label almost any of the attacks demons launch against humans as *oppression*. Use of this term is extremely broad. To say a demon is oppressing us may indicate that he is intensifying some chronic physical illness, creating situations that are difficult to endure, dragging us deeper into despondency and despair, etc. Or an oppressing demon may create a situation in which we suffer injustice and become angry, thus leading us into sin. The demon's goal is to prod us to act out in some sinful way, rather than choose to turn the situation over to God for Him to resolve.

While the phrase *demonic possession* suggests demonic control of an individual, the phrase *demonic oppression* suggests influence. This influence can be exerted from outside the person, by manipulating a situation to cause frustration, anger or fear. When possible, demons prefer to manipulate from within an individual's personality, intensifying ungodly beliefs and emotions that can lead to sinful acts.

Chester and Betsy Kylstra, in *Restoring the Foundations: An Integrated Approach to Healing Ministry* (Proclaiming His Word, 2001), specify the various ways they have observed evil spirits' influence on the three aspects of humanity—spirit, soul (meaning mind, will and emotions) and body. As the Kylstras demonstrate, symptoms of demonic manipulation of the body may include things like illness and excessive appetite (such as for food). Demonic oppression of the mind shows itself in tormenting or compulsive thoughts. Oppression of the will includes symptoms like the inability to follow through on decisions we know must be made. Demons' influence on the emotions is likely when emotional states such as fear or grief become exaggerated. And symptoms of the ability to oppress the spirit include instances of people who seem spiritually lethargic or full of doubt. These as well as other symptoms often indicate demonic oppression.

Ron Phillips, in his book *Everyone's Guide to Demons and Spiritual Warfare* (Charisma, 2010), also offers visual markers of demonic operation. He explains that demons exercise oppression through the ways they operate in a person's life—naming fourteen symptoms that include "incapacity for normal living," "personality changes," "terrible inner anguish" and "doctrinal error." This brings home the point that demons can function outside or within an individual's personality.

When we compare these symptoms to numerous others outlined in deliverance literature, we realize how broadly the idea of demonic oppression is applied. Not only is there a wide range of behaviors at least partially symptomatic of demonic oppression, but also there is a wide range of intensity within those behaviors. Personality changes, for instance, as Phillips points out, may be mild or may swing into radical or destructive behavior. We all grow and change; some personality changes are natural evidence of personal growth. But when the changes have negative impact on the individual or on his or her relationships with others, oppression by evil spirits is likely.

When reading deliverance literature or listening to messages on deliverance, be aware that the phrase *demonic oppression* is used with great flexibility. Yet the particular application of the term in any given situation is crucial if the deliverance minister is to find appropriate ways to free the oppressed individual from Satan's influence.

Demonic Possession

"Demon possession" is a truly unfortunate translation of the Greek term *diamonizomai*. While this rendering of the Greek occurs over and over in the gospels, it is far from the best translation. The Greek term might better be rendered as "demonized" or "has a demon."

There are significant reasons why we should not speak of demon possession. First, the term *possession* implies control, as though a demon is submerging the individual's personality and acting through that person's body against the individual's will. In fact, demons almost never gain "control" of a person. Demons might *like* to have that kind of control. But humans do not surrender their freedom of choice that easily.

When Satan manipulated Eve and then Adam into rebelling against God, I suspect he imagined that humans would ally themselves with him and his purposes, just as the angels who followed him in the great rebellion had done. But that did not happen. In stating the consequences of Satan's effort to enlist humans, the Creator told Satan that He would put "enmity" between Satan and the woman's seed. Yes, some do commit to Satan. But for most of us there is healthy suspicion of Satan and reluctance to trust him, which keeps us from total submission. We are no more eager to commit to Satan than we are to commit to God. We humans just naturally want to go our own way rather than submit to either God or Satan. Thus, "enmity," a deep-seated suspicion and underlying hostility toward the supernatural, which makes us hesitant to commit ourselves to the Creator, also protects us from domination by the evil one. We certainly can be and are influenced by Satan's minions. But controlled? Seldom.

Second, the phrase *demon possession* is unfortunate in that it seems to release us from any responsibility for demonic influences in our lives. While we humans are undoubtedly vulnerable to Satan's schemes, and often are victims of choices made by others, there seems always to be some level of personal responsibility when demons establish a foothold in our lives. This does not mean that we make an intentional choice to let demons in. But I believe there is always some responsibility on our part for the entry or continued presence of evil spirits in our lives.

For both these reasons, speaking of and picturing demonic activity as being possessed is unfortunate. And it is scary. Who wants to be under the control of a demon?

What term provides a more accurate picture of the meaning of demonization than "possession"? I believe *hitchhiking*. In the 1930s I enjoyed hitchhiking on my dad's car. In those days cars had running boards. These were six-inch strips along each side of the car that a person would step on to enter the vehicle. But if Dad rolled the car window down, a kid like me could also ride on a running board, holding tightly to the frame of the open window.

This strikes me as a better picture of demonization than is possession. Somehow we rolled down a window, giving a demon a place to grab hold. And he or they jumped aboard. They are holding on tight, eager to make as much trouble for us as possible.

I like the hitchhiker image a lot better than the possession image. There is no question of demonic control. For all intents and purposes demons are simply clinging to us, determined to go along for the ride. Sure, a demon might reach inside the window and tug on the steering wheel. One might even cause an accident or two. But control? No.

One other thing is wrong with the image of possession. Possession makes it seem that demons are so tightly fused with us that they are almost impossible to get rid of. But it is not difficult to picture a hitchhiking demon being given a good shove and landing in a heap alongside the road. That is a pretty accurate description of what happens when we command a demon to leave in Jesus' name. The demons *are* expelled.

I like the running board image for another reason, too. If my dad kept the car window rolled up, there was no place for me to cling to and no way I could stay on that running board. If you and I keep our figurative spiritual windows rolled up, there is no place for demons to grab hold of and gain access to our lives.

Demonic Stronghold

There are a number of references to strongholds in the Old Testament. In Old Testament times the stronghold was the core of a fortified position. It was the safest and strongest position possible, often at the center of many layers of stone and other defensive constructions. The psalmists praised God frequently as the stronghold to which they could retreat in time of danger.

There is only one reference to strongholds in the New Testament. This is found in 2 Corinthians. While clearly picking up the imagery of the Old Testament and its culture, this reference to strongholds is unique. Paul writes:

> Though we live in the world, we do not wage war as the world does. The weapons we fight with are not the weapons of the world. On the contrary, they have divine power to demolish strongholds. We demolish arguments and every pretension that sets itself up against the knowledge of God, and we take captive every thought to make it obedient to Christ.
>
> 2 Corinthians 10:3–5

This concept of a spiritual stronghold that must be torn down is today extremely significant in deliverance ministry. Our understanding of just what demonic strongholds are has been developed from this passage.

Paul here pictures demonic strongholds as "pretensions" that set themselves up "against the knowledge of God." Generally pretensions are considered to be ungodly beliefs. These are beliefs that distort our image of God or corrupt our concept of ourselves as God's children. An insecure woman, for example, might view God as judgmental and punishing, when this is not His nature at all. A man who struggles with self-confidence might view himself as utterly inadequate, a nothing, someone who will never succeed at anything in life. The truth is that we were created in God's image, and that, in Christ, we were refashioned and given the Holy Spirit to enable us to live lives that are pleasing to God. Christ has provided all the resources we need to reach our potential as godly individuals who can overcome evil with good. Both of these are examples of ungodly beliefs that do not square with Scripture's revelation of the nature of God or our own nature as individuals created in His image.

Ungodly beliefs are difficult to attack. They are often at the core of many of the presenting symptoms of demonization. In this sense they truly are strongholds, the last and most powerful defensive position that can be taken by demons when we seek to cast them out. Even when the steps of deliverance have been dealt with—we have named the demon associated with the oppression; we have removed the legal ground including forgiving anyone who caused the hurt; we have commanded the demon to leave in Jesus' name—frequently there are still demons behind the walls of a stronghold that are not obvious to us. Paul makes it clear that we have divine power to demolish those strongholds. Under the guidance of the Holy Spirit we can demolish arguments and tear down every pretension that sets itself up against the knowledge of God.

But before we can tear down demonic strongholds, we need to deal with what the person seeking deliverance sees as his or her most significant problems. This is one of the reasons why this particular issue is cast in the framework of a stronghold, for strongholds are the key defensive position often entrenched behind other problems caused by other demons. How then do we demolish demonic strongholds?

The answer is found in the 2 Corinthians passage. Again, the demons building the stronghold marshal arguments and pretensions designed to distort our image of God and of who we are in Christ. We demolish these tools of evil spirits by presenting the truth as God has clearly revealed it in Scripture. The Holy Spirit will take God's Word and use it to demolish the ungodly and faulty images we have of God and of ourselves, and gradually to embed the truth in our hearts and lives.

In Scripture's terms, God's Word has the power to take captive (and captivate) our hearts, and lead us to respond appropriately to God as we discover the depths of His love and commitment to us. God's Word will also change our perception of ourselves, so that we might discover the deeply loved and Spirit-enabled persons we really are.

It is very important in deliverance ministry to realize that there are strongholds marked by ungodly and unbiblical beliefs that exist at the core of many who seek deliverance. We will need to be sensitive to the Holy Spirit's leading as to just when and how to attack these strongholds, but one thing we can do to equip ourselves is to memorize the Scriptures that affirm and display God's love, and that present every believer as a significant member of the Body of Christ. We are persons who are enabled by the Spirit of God to please Him in every way.

See *Strongholds (Ungodly Beliefs)*.

Devil

The Bible identifies two primary names of the enemy of mankind: *Satan*, which means "adversary," and *the devil* (*diábolos*), which means "one who slanders or accuses." As a powerful angel created by God, he was overwhelmed by a warped desire to take God's place. His initial rebellion included many of the heavenly host—spirit beings who chose to follow him.

It is clear from Scripture that Satan, although defeated in that first battle, continues to exercise great power in this world. He is called the "ruler of the kingdom of the air" in Ephesians 2:2 and is at work in all those who are disobedient to God. Despite his powers and the strategies that he uses so successfully to deceive humanity, he was defeated in every confrontation he had with Jesus (e.g., Matthew 4:1–11; Luke 11:14–22; 13:10–16).

During this present age Satan can be seen as the commander of the great army of demons who are intent on thwarting God's intentions for humankind. Often these attacks by demons or evil spirits are focused on individuals, especially believers, in an attempt to keep us from bringing glory to God. At the same time Satan and his minions are focused on the corruption of human cultures—they are intent on bringing chaos to our societies and corrupting the good that God intends in bringing people together in marriage, families, neighborhoods and nations. Anyone who has observed the decline of American society over the last forty years must realize that Satan is extremely active and influential on this larger, cultural stage.

While we might view Satan as the commander-in-chief of demonic hordes, we need to be clear about the relationship between Satan and demons. Satan is the most powerful of all demons. Other demons are subject to him. But both Satan and demons do and can make choices. It would be a mistake to believe that the choices every demon makes are specifically directed by Satan. What Satan has done is establish what we today call "the rules of engagement." Satan establishes the goals, develops the strategies and to some extent guides tactics. But in our war with evil, individual demons are free to act within this framework as much as they choose. Both Satan and demons have free will, but they are free only to do evil. There is no chance any redeeming quality will be found in either Satan or demons.

While it is possible, I am unaware of any reliable report in deliverance ministry that Satan himself was directly involved in possessing or oppressing an individual. This is something we can be thankful for, as even the archangel Michael in a confrontation with Satan, rather than rebuke him directly, said, "The Lord rebuke you!" (Jude 1:9).

While at present Satan conducts what we might call an "underground war" against God and humankind, and especially believers, the New Testament predicts a day when Satan will lead another great open rebellion (see 2 Thessalonians 2). After this final attempt to overthrow God (see Revelation 20:7–9), God will put an end to Satan and to the evil he represents, casting him into what Revelation calls a lake of burning sulfur to "be tormented day and night for ever and ever" (Revelation 20:10).

While Satan and his followers have significant powers to operate against believers, we need to remember that we are facing a defeated enemy, one who is well aware of his impending doom. Our goal in the struggle is to live for God's glory, choosing what is good and right, motivated by an ever-growing love for Jesus. And should we be attacked by Satan's demons, we need to rest assured that in the name of Jesus those demons who are oppressing us can be cast out.

Discernment

Usually by *discernment* deliverance ministers mean the ability to recognize the presence of evil spirits. This recognition might come through observation of symptoms often associated with demonization. At times deliverance ministers view discernment primarily as a gift, given by the Holy Spirit, which enables them to sense the presence of evil spirits and at times even to identify a specific demon. At times discernment includes guidance by the Holy Spirit as to how to deal with an infesting spirit during a deliverance session.

Dissociative Identity Disorder

See *Alter.*

Dreams and Visions

The Old Testament reports a number of kinds of dreams. God used ordinary dreams to reveal information (see Job 7:14; Ecclesiastes 5:3). Numbers 12:6 states, "When a prophet of the LORD is among you, I reveal myself to him in visions, I speak to him in dreams." Pagan prophets, however, who were intent on leading Israel astray, also claimed that dreams and visions gave authority to their teachings. Deuteronomy 13:3 warns, "You must not listen to the words of that prophet or dreamer."

Interestingly, there is no reference in Scripture to revelatory dreams following the birth of Christ. God has given us His Holy

Spirit to teach us and to lead us. While He remains free to communicate to individuals in dreams, we must also remain aware that Satan's demons have that same ability.

Evil Spirit

See *Demon*.

Fallen Angels

Fallen angels are those who followed Satan in his great initial rebellion. Today we know them as demons and evil spirits, as they are typically identified in deliverance ministries.

See *Demon* and *Devil*.

Familial Spirit

The adjective *familial* refers to anything that occurs or tends to recur in a family. Thus familial spirits are those that seem to associate themselves with a particular family.

We are all aware that traits and characteristics of parents are frequently transmitted to their children, and they recur generation after generation. It is likely that if a parent bullies or abuses a child, that same tendency in the parenting style will be repeated in his offspring. Most deliverance ministers find recurring family traits to be an indication of possible demonization.

Chester and Betsy Kylstra, in *Restoring the Foundations*, provide a chart listing sins that are found frequently within family lines. While they attribute these to curses, each is related to behaviors and character traits that can be learned from the behavior modeled by the parents as the child matures. Examples from their list are "inferiority," "greed," "not caring for children" and "rebellion."

Since traits like these can be developed through the emotional and spiritual environment of the home, it is a fair question to ask if familial evil spirits truly are involved when we note such characteristics in someone seeking deliverance.

In asking this question we should keep one thing in mind. Demons do not create character traits, but the traits can and do serve as entry points into a person's life. There the demons will do all they can to intensify the problem, thus making it even more likely that the next generation will reproduce these sins of the parents. When we see a pattern repeating itself within family lines, we should definitely consider the possibility of demonic involvement.

Many deliverance ministers believe that in dealing with familial spirits an element should be added to the deliverance process. This element is what is called in deliverance ministry *breaking soul ties*. The nature of soul ties and how deliverance ministers seek to break them is discussed under the entry "Soul Ties."

More and more research has demonstrated the impact of home and family on the development of even the youngest children. It is extremely unlikely that Satan's demons would be ignorant of opportunities that the sins embedded in a parent's character provide for gaining entry into their children's lives.

Familiar Spirit

Scripture's attitude toward those who consult a familiar spirit is utterly clear. Leviticus 20:27 commands: "A man also or woman that hath a familiar spirit, or that is a wizard, shall surely be put to death" (AKJV). The reference here is to a medium or spiritist who claims the ability to open a link between the living and the dead. Webster's dictionary describes the *familiar spirit*, which in the original means a "household servant," as either "a spirit (or demon) who serves an individual" or "the spirit of a dead person evoked by a medium to provide information and guidance to the living." Of the two, Scripture is clear that familiar spirits are demons; they are not defined as spirits of dead persons who communicate with living loved ones through the agency of the medium.

Those who claim to be mediums typically offer the service of contacting the dead; a small group of people may gather and follow the guidance of the medium, who then consults a familiar spirit. This practice of contacting a familiar spirit is repeatedly condemned in Scripture, identified as "defiling" and in Old Testament times worthy of death. One of the most serious consequences of consulting a medium with a familiar spirit is that this places us voluntarily in contact with the spirit world and opens us to demonization. Engaging in any and every kind of occult practice opens a door into our personalities to evil spirits.

Generational Curses

When those in deliverance ministry speak of generational curses, they are usually referring to the same symptoms that identify a familial spirit. The assumption that the cause is a curse is based on verses like Exodus 34:7, which says that God "punishes the children and their children for the sin of the fathers to the third and fourth generation." Many in deliverance ministry view the sins of parents and grandparents that are repeated in their children's lives as a consequence of a curse. Others view repeating sins as natural, a reflection of the way that all children tend to take on traits and attitudes of their parents.

As noted above, those who believe that it is necessary to deal with familial spirits and generational curses approach the deliverance process in a slightly different way from other deliverance ministers.

See *Curses* and *Sins of the Fathers*.

Healing (Inner) and Deliverance

Most deliverance ministers agree that inner healing is a significant element in deliverance. There is, however, little or no agreement when it comes to the vocabulary that they use. For some, inner healing is deliverance from what they call "ungodly beliefs," distorted ideas about God or themselves. For some it is the healing of memories or the healing of emotions. For others it is "breaking down strongholds"—areas in the personality or character where sinful actions or attitudes dominate. At the same time, whatever vocabulary is used, there is generally a common understanding of what inner healing involves.

Most see the source of the damage that requires inner healing as some sort of trauma, most frequently, but not necessarily, experienced in childhood. This trauma may be physical, as from beatings or injury. The trauma may be psychological, such as public ridicule from a teacher over a school assignment, or frequent verbal abuse by someone who is important to the individual, such as a parent. All too often some form of sexual abuse lies at the heart of the damage.

The impact of the trauma may vary widely among individuals. Some who were beaten or otherwise physically abused as children grow up to become angry and hostile adults who abuse their own children in turn. Others who endured similar physical abuse respond in completely different ways, such as becoming compassionate and caring adults who minister to the abused. Likewise, some who were verbally abused as children develop a distorted self-image, leading to the belief that they can never amount to anything or succeed in anything they might be willing to risk trying. Others overcome those feelings of inferiority from verbal abuse and determine to make a positive difference in the world. While the source and nature of trauma can vary widely, so the impact of trauma can also vary widely. The same experience can have little lasting impact on some individuals and a devastating and destructive impact on others.

This phenomenon, sometimes identified as a "trauma-response event" because it involves a response to some sort of trauma, is assumed to lie at the root of the damage, which requires inner healing. Whatever the terminology used by a deliverance minister, most assume that some trauma-response event is behind the damaged emotions, corrupted beliefs and wounded hearts that require healing if we are to experience the abundant and godly life that Christ provides for believers.

Approaches to inner healing ministry vary widely. For some, inner healing is essentially a prayer ministry. The deliverance minister, after identifying the source and nature of the individual's problem, will pray for freedom from the impact of earlier trauma-response experiences, encourage the individual to forgive anyone who played a part in the experience, and replace any negative thoughts or emotions with godly counterparts.

For others, inner healing is closely linked with deliverance. This approach assumes that demonic involvement is possible or likely. The deliverance minister seeks to identify the source and nature of an individual's problem, dealing with any sinful thoughts or attitudes that are blocking release from the impact of the trauma-response pattern. Then the minister commands any demons associated with the trauma or its impact to leave the individual.

Each approach has its dangers and drawbacks. Those who see the impact of the trauma-response experience as completely natural are likely to miss any demons who are present and fail in the attempt to bring total healing. Those who see the impact of trauma-response experience as natural and normal, but assume it has opened a door to a demonic presence, may see demons that actually are not present. In this case they might attempt to "cast out" an emotion or a belief as a demonic component, causing additional harm rather than bringing healing. A more balanced approach recognizes the fact that while a response of emotional trauma is natural, demons can use this response against us.

Most deliverance ministers see three ways that demons take advantage of the trauma-response pattern: (1) Demons use a trauma-response pattern as an entry point into an individual's life. A sinful response to trauma is viewed as opening the door for demons and as providing a basis for demons to claim a right to an individual's life; (2) Demons strengthen the person's natural response. If a person's response is fear, for instance, demons intensify the fear to the point that the individual is unwilling to take any risks at all; (3) Demons take advantage of the individual's trauma response and build a "stronghold"—constructing a sort of fortress within the individual, and strengthening the emotions, beliefs and behaviors that lie at the core of the sinful practices encouraged by these particular demons.

While each individual ministering inner healing will have his or her own approach, the following is a description of a somewhat typical scenario that involves both inner healing and deliverance from demonization. The approach described is essentially a co-operative one. At a minimum, the person seeking help should (1) want to be rid of hidden demons, (2) forgive those whose actions may have opened the door to the demonization, and (3) be committed to turning away from any sins associated with the demonization.

Let's assume that you are a deliverance minister. A man comes to you who says he loses control when he gets angry and fears he will harm his wife or children. In talking with him you discover that he was the victim of his father's rage as a child. You realize that a spirit of anger or a spirit of violence could have entered his life through his father's brutality.

You begin by asking him to choose to forgive his father for the sin perpetrated against him.

If the man is also angry with God for permitting his father to abuse him, you encourage him to "forgive" the Lord as well. Remember, we cannot blame God for permitting painful experiences that are always in some way connected to our own sins or others' sins. You explain to him that God loves him and has always loved him, but does not overrule human choices. You assure him that God hurt with him as he was abused.

You then explain that the man must take responsibility for any resentment or anger against his father, confess those sins and accept God's forgiveness, just as he confesses and accepts responsibility for his own abuse of his wife and children.

Following this work of inner healing, you address the spirit of anger or spirit of violence or any other evil spirit that seems to be present. By forgiving his father and confessing his own sin, the man has removed what some call the "legal basis" for any demon's attachment to his personality, and you can now command each demon in Jesus' name to leave the man, to never return to him or his family.

With the spirits of rage and violence cast out, you bless the man with calm and with patience as you continue praying for him.

You then can go on to deal with other related issues, such as addiction to pornography, etc. Since the man reveals that this is a pattern in his life, you focus on spirits of lust and addiction and follow the same process. You seek to identify events that could have given evil spirits access, such as early sexual abuse or perhaps repeatedly sampling pornography or sexual promiscuity.

Again you help the demonized man deal with the damage through forgiveness, confession and repudiation of the underlying sin. You minister forgiveness for the guilt and shame he feels. At this point you command these evil spirits to leave in Jesus' name, using the authority God has given His people. Then you bless the man with purity and with the joy of sex within marriage, which is God's gift to human beings.

Note that the process for dealing with inner healing and deliverance together contains four vital elements: (1) Identify the root of the problem and its sources; (2) Deal with these problems, with a focus on confession, forgiveness and repudiation; (3) Cast out the demons in Jesus' name; (4) Bless the individual with the opposite traits of those energized by demons.

While some in deliverance ministry prefer to deal with inner healing *after* casting out any demons present, others wish to deal with inner healing *first*, believing that this weakens the ability of any demons present to resist. Most take an integrative approach, like the one described above, and look to the Holy Spirit to guide the process.

Healing (Physical) and Deliverance

It should be clear to anyone who glances through the gospels that there is a link between physical healing and deliverance from demons. Healing and deliverance are spoken of in the same sentence in Matthew 4:24, which tells us that the people of Syria brought to Jesus "all who were ill with various diseases, those suffering severe pain, the [demonized]." Matthew 8:16 tells us that when "evening came, many who were [demonized] were brought to him, and he drove out the spirits with a word and healed all the sick." Matthew 9:32–34 tells the story of a demonized man who was unable to speak: "When the demon was driven out, the man who had been mute spoke. The crowd was amazed and said, 'Nothing like this has ever been seen in Israel'" (verse 33). Luke 8:2–3 describes "some women who had been cured of evil spirits and diseases: Mary (called Magdalene) from whom seven demons had come out; Joanna the wife of Cuza . . . ; Susanna; and many others."

It is not surprising that a relationship between demonization and illness should exist. While Scripture addresses the perspectives of body, soul and spirit, we are a unity. What happens to us physically has significant influence on our psychological states, as well as on the way we relate to God and others. Similarly, damage to the soul, as by trauma experienced in early childhood or later, is well known to affect physical health. The gospel records affirm that demons cause or enhance specific disabilities. A clear example of this is found in Mark 9:25, where Jesus addressed a demon as "you deaf and mute spirit." When Jesus cast this spirit out, the man was able both to hear and speak. The realization that demonization has some impact on our physical or psychological well-being is almost inescapable, though the nature of that impact is likely to vary, as is the intensity.

Even though a relationship between demonization and physical health is evident, trying to explore it is difficult for one important reason: While the New Testament is clear about how to cast out demons, there are no similar instructions concerning healing. I suggest that this is because demons are sentient individuals, living beings with all the capacities of humans. When we command an evil spirit in the name of Jesus, that spirit hears, understands and is compelled against its will to leave the person it has infected. Diseases and disabilities are not sentient individuals. Diseases cannot hear, cannot understand, cannot make choices and cannot respond as persons to any commands we might give.

There are also no specifics about who might be gifted to serve in the area of healing. When Christ sent His twelve disciples out to minister, He "gave them authority to drive out evil spirits and to heal every disease and sickness" (Matthew 10:1). Luke 9:1 reports the same dual commissioning: "When Jesus had called the Twelve together, he gave them power and authority to drive out all demons and to cure diseases." But there is no hint in Scripture that all believers are commissioned and able to heal, while all believers do have the authority to cast out demons. Certainly, there is no indication in the New Testament that the ability to heal parallels the authority Jesus gives us over demons. What we do know about healing is that 1 Corinthians 12:9 states that *some* believers are given the spiritual gift of healing. It is also clear from this passage that the gift of healing, like other gifts distributed by the Holy

173

Spirit, is given to "each one, just as he [the Holy Spirit] determines" (1 Corinthians 12:11).

The fact that demons can affect physical and mental well-being leads to assumptions about healing that are sometimes not borne out. In larger deliverance and healing rallies, for instance, immediate healings are viewed as indications that demons were manifesting in the sickness and serve as proof that the demons have been expelled. Too often such sudden and complete "healings" turn out to be "hysterical" rather than real. The woman who drops her crutches to walk off the stage may very well collapse later. More typically, physical healing following deliverance is characterized by a slower and more natural-seeming recovery. Still, numerous contemporary testimonies show that actual healings have taken place following the casting out of evil spirits.

How then should we approach physical healing and deliverance? First we need to recognize that there is a strong link between demonization and many sicknesses and disabilities. Second we need to realize that whenever a physical illness is made worse by demons, we must focus our efforts on casting out the demons. Depending on the nature of the connection between demons and our physical problems, we may in some cases expect to see physical recovery. In unusual cases this recovery might be immediate; in other cases it might be gradual and seemingly "natural."

Jesus can and does heal today. Casting out demons clearly is linked to deliverance. But deliverance does not guarantee healing.

Inner Healing

See *Healing (Inner) and Deliverance.*

Legal Ground

The phrase *legal ground* keeps coming up in a discussion of deliverance ministry. The phrase refers to the fact that demons seem to require some basis for being present in a person's life. While a few people will consciously invite demons into their lives for some purpose of their own, in most cases the doors open to demons unintentionally. Yet demons do need to have a door opened for them. They apparently cannot simply infest anyone they please. An open door gives demons the right to be present. This, a "right to be present," is what deliverance ministers mean by legal ground.

There are four primary avenues that deliverance ministers believe demons use to establish a right to be present in an individual's life.

1. Trafficking with the occult: Deuteronomy 18 clearly forbids God's people from becoming involved in any occult practice. To seek contact with the spirit world other than seeking relationship with the Lord constitutes an open invitation to demons and provides legal ground for their presence in one's life.

2. Habitual personal sin: In the same way the habitual practice of sin can provide access to demons and serve as legal ground, giving them a right to be present in our lives. The sins that provide access need not be the baser physical actions we usually equate with disobedience to God, but can include something as "harmless" as gossip.

3. Trauma: Dramatic events, particularly during childhood, can stimulate emotional reactions that also seem to provide demons with an open door. These reactions may include anger, fear, shame and guilt, which typically lead to self-cursing and

self-hatred. These results definitely serve as legal ground for a demonic presence.

4. Sins of the Fathers: Many deliverance ministers consider ancestral sins and curses as a fourth category that provides demons with the right to be present in a person's life.

The person receiving ministry needs to cooperate with what many deliverance ministers believe is the first step: removing the legal grounds. This is done by identifying the avenues through which the demon or demons entered, by confessing any sins that have been involved and by forgiving any individuals who had a part in helping to create the open door for demons.

Magick

There are 23 references to magic and magicians in the Old Testament. The spelling of *magick* distinguishes occult action from the sleight-of-hand tricks practiced by illusionists. Magick, through which an individual attempts to tap into supernatural powers in an effort to cause effects that he or she wishes, has an ancient history. Archaeological evidence shows that the ancients used a multitude of curses and protective spells.

Today many of those who practice magick make a distinction between black magick, which is intended to harm another person, and white magick, which they say is used only to benefit themselves or other individuals. Ultimately, however, there is no real distinction, as any form of magick is an attempt to harness forces in the spiritual universe to have impact on experiences in our world. Any such attempt is strictly forbidden in Scripture and, as with other occult practices, opens a doorway through which evil spirits may enter an individual's life.

Perhaps not surprisingly many black magick services are offered on the Internet. One site, selling retribution and curse spells for $39.95, suggests the purchaser "even the score with that evil person," claim "an eye for an eye with that wicked person" or "have the jinx on me removed at once." The site suggests that for another $39.95 the spell can be cast twice, to increase its power.

Deliverance ministers take magick spells seriously, recognizing the reality of a spirit world filled with hostile demons. When spells are recognized, their influence is broken by the power of Christ.

See *Curses*.

Manifestations

In deliverance ministry a manifestation is an obvious expression of a demon's presence in an individual's life. Despite the delight of those in the film industry in showing obviously strange and supernatural activities, demonic manifestations are not the norm. Manifestations confirm the presence of demons, something that demons definitely do not want to do. Demons like to remain hidden and operate in the dark.

Typically manifestations will occur during the final stages of an exorcism. The demon realizes that he has been identified and no longer can disguise himself in the person as an overly emotional individual, or mad, or the victim of some illness. On the other hand, manifestations such as levitation, throwing the individual about or shrieking in an unknown language might be used to frighten or distract the deliverance minister from completing the process of exorcism. In this case it is good to remember that Jesus is Lord and the demon is subject to Christ. It is best simply to remain calm and to command the demon to stop his exhibitions.

Medium

See *Channeling* and *Familiar Spirit*.

Naming Demons

See *Deliverance Ministry*.

Occult

We human beings were created with an awareness that a spiritual universe lies alongside our own. With that awareness comes hunger to experience what that universe offers. God has always intended that our hunger be satisfied through personal relationship with Him. Tragically, humankind turned to other avenues to contact this spiritual universe. The meaning of the word *occult* is "hidden" or "secret." In deliverance ministry *the occult* refers to attempts to gain knowledge or control supernaturally, through the influence of inhabitants of the spirit world. Occult practices by which people seek knowledge or guidance include the use of Ouija boards, tarot cards, astrological charts, palm reading, and the consultation of psychics and mediums. Occult practices by which people seek to gain some control over events or persons include witchcraft, casting spells, sorcery and seeking out a spirit guide.

Many non-Christians assume that the spirit world is inhabited by gods, goddesses, the spirits of humans who have died, angels, demons, totems and animal spirits. These are assumed to be benevolently inclined and eager to help those who contact them. The Bible makes it clear that any spirit beings contacted through occult means are demons, followers of Satan, who hate and are committed to harming human beings. Scripture absolutely forbids reliance on any occult practice for any purpose, whether seeking knowledge, healing of an illness, or influencing events or people. The key passage that takes this prohibition and lists a variety of occult practices is Deuteronomy 18:9–13:

> Do not learn to imitate the detestable ways of the nations there. Let no one be found among you who sacrifices his son or daughter in the fire, who practices divination or sorcery, interprets omens, engages in witchcraft, or cast spells, or who is a medium or spiritist or who consults the dead. Anyone who does these things is detestable to the LORD, and because of these detestable practices the LORD your God will drive out those nations from before you. You must be blameless before the LORD your God.

A similar emphasis is found in Leviticus 20:2–7, and repeated in the New Testament in Galatians 5:20, Revelation 21:8 and elsewhere.

The commandments against involvement in occult practices have been established for our benefit. To initiate contact with an evil spirit provides that spirit with legal ground to attach himself to one's personality. Those in deliverance ministry agree that the most difficult demons to expel are occult spirits. Engaging in any occult practice opens a person to demonic oppression.

Especially in this area it is vital to undercut any legal ground that demons claim for their presence in a person's life. This involves a process of acknowledgment and confession of responsibility, complete and utter repudiation of occult activities, the destruction of all objects associated with occult practices, and forgiveness of any who led the individual into the occult world. I also recommend that these steps be followed with the public confession of Christ as Lord and the spoken commitment to love, serve and obey Him.

Oppression

See *Demonic Oppression*.

Personal Responsibility

One of the questions often raised in deliverance ministry is, How responsible is an individual for his or her own demonization? When demonization results from involvement with the occult or from habitual sin, it is difficult to argue that the person has not opened the door. Even in cases where the conditions for demonization stem from the sins of others, such as physical or sexual abuse, that wounded individual still makes personal choices in the wake of those abuses.

Most in deliverance ministry today recognize that there is always some responsibility on the part of the demonized individual. If the person has not opened a door to demonization, that one has at the very least not kept the door closed, by choosing to behave in harmony with lies demons tell.

It is helpful here to remember something unique about sin. Each of the basic Greek words that express the biblical concept of sin refers to standards that have been established by God, built into human nature and revealed through Scripture. One word group portrays *sin* as a "twisting of the standard." Another portrays it as "rebellion against the standard." Each of these involves the will. The third word group—the most common—simply portrays sin as "falling short of the standard." Here we human beings remain responsible for our failures, for Scripture reminds us that "all have sinned and fall short of the glory of God" (Romans 3:23). We are responsible, but our failure does not necessarily involve intent.

We would be wrong to accuse every victim of demonization of being intentionally responsible. We can, however, affirm that in every case we bear some responsibility simply by the fact of our vulnerability. The good news is that even without deliverance ministry, believers can grow in faith and limit the ability of demons to disrupt our lives.

Physical Healing

See *Healing (Physical) and Deliverance.*

Possession

See *Demonic Possession.*

Power Encounter

The simplest way to describe *power encounter* is "direct and open conflict between God and the powers of Satan." We have a number of examples of power encounters in Scripture. A prime example is the Exodus story. Pharaoh had complete confidence in the powers of the gods of Egypt and nothing but contempt for the God of the Hebrew slaves. Yet when these two supernatural powers went head to head, each god of Egypt was crushed and defeated by the God of Israel. Finally even Pharaoh had to confess that the Lord is God and release the slaves. And when he changed his mind and set out in pursuit of the Israelites, the army that he led was destroyed. There was no question that in this power encounter, "large-G" God was dominant.

We see similar results in contemporary confrontations described by many missionaries who face demonic powers in their fields of labor. As Christians carry the Gospel to peoples ensnared by paganism, the witch doctors or other spiritual leaders of the people usually marshal their resources to oppose the bearers of the Christian message. At times this sparks an open challenge. Because the gods of the pagans are real, and because Satan is intent on thwarting God's purposes in bringing eternal life and blessing to all, the power encounter often leads to manifestations of the demons' presence. One missionary describes it as "a showdown of sorts." But it always leads to the defeat of the pagan god at the hands of those who rely on Jesus' authority. Typically power encounters in this context initiate mass conversions to Christ.

At times we witness power encounters in movements closer to home. These typically draw much attention, especially in certain segments of the Church. When we do see evidence of power encounters, most deliverance ministers will praise God and give Him the glory. It is important for all of us to remember that the power and the authority belong to Jesus alone. While we may be His agents in bringing freedom, we have no basis for claiming credit or for lifting ourselves above any other believers.

In a very real sense, we can call each casting out of evil spirits a power encounter, though a hidden one. God does work wonders in human lives, and while they may be done in secret here and now, they will redound to His glory eternally.

Prophecy

Some in deliverance ministry today identify themselves as prophets. To evaluate this use of the language we need to understand the roots of the concept in the Old and New Testaments.

The primary word for *prophet* in the Old Testament means "spokesman" or "speaker." Thus an Old Testament prophet was a messenger who was authorized to speak for God. While a prophet's words were generally predictive, meaning they provided information about the near or distant future, the prophet's primary ministry was to offer correction to the people of his or her own generation.

The prophecies recorded in the Old Testament were distinct from other prophecies because they were considered to be God's authoritative revelation to His chosen people. Some are clearly words for all believers for all time, but even prophecies spoken for the welfare of particular kings or armies had a part, ultimately, in helping to fulfill God's redemptive plan. God spoke through many prophets to give guidance or direction, but only those prophecies included in the canon of Scripture were set apart as revelation of His broader will and purposes for all of His people.

Many of the Old Testament prophecies are predictive, dealing with future events. Where these prophecies have already been fulfilled, the prophets' predictions have been fulfilled literally. We can be confident that the written prophecies concerning what still lies in the future will also be fulfilled in the same clear and unmistakable way.

The New Testament meaning expressed in the Greek word *prophetes* is clearly built on the Old Testament concept. Prophets are messengers who speak for God, sometimes to individuals and sometimes to the contemporary Church. At times these messages are predictive (see Acts 21:10–11). Yet the primary focus of New Testament prophecies is stated in 1 Corinthians 14:3: "Everyone who prophesies speaks to [people] for their strengthening, encouragement and comfort."

We can say then that the focus of the New Testament prophet is on "personal prophecies" rather than on national predictive prophecy. Prophets ministered to individuals and their church communities, and what they said is not revelation in the sense that the prophetic words of the Old Testament are revelation from God for the whole Church. In *Restoring the Foundations*, the Kylstras comment:

> In a sense, everything involved with communication from God is prophecy. This is true as long as we define "prophecy" as God speaking a word personally to an individual. This is not a significant communication used during the ministry process. Sometimes, however, as part of the opening and closing, the Holy Spirit in one of the ministers offers the person encouragement, understanding, insight, and comfort.

It is important to be wary of how a deliverance minister is using the concepts of *prophet* and *prophecy*. God does minister to us through the words and encouragement of our fellow believers. When the contemporary prophet focuses on predictions or prescriptions, however, this focus, although there may be infrequent times when God shares something of the future of individuals, is out of harmony with the New Testament revelation.

We need to remember always that God has given each believer the Holy Spirit to enable us to interpret and apply the written Word for ourselves. It is to Scripture and the Spirit that the Christian looks for guidance and encouragement. When anyone claims to have a prophetic gift that goes beyond the examples provided in the New Testament, we need to be suspicious of those claims. Certainly we must remember that if any prophecy is in conflict with the written Word, that prophecy is not valid. Scripture is our final authority.

Satan

See *Devil*.

Sexual Abuse

Some researchers claim that as many as a third of girls and women will be sexually abused by age thirty and that many boys will also suffer sexual abuse. Whatever the actual number—and it is both large and growing—sexual abuse has devastating effects on the victims. The damage done to one's self-image and to the ability to relate to the opposite sex cannot be overestimated.

One unmentioned impact of sexual abuse is that frequently it opens the door to demonization. The trauma of the experience, especially when the abuse is repeated, and the emotions the abuse engenders seem to attract demons. Those emotions and thoughts provide a foothold for demons within the victim's personality. While we cannot understand how an innocent individual can fall victim to demons through another's sin, this is exactly what happens.

The best way to reconcile this is to understand the biblical concept of evil. In the Old Testament a single word group, based on the Hebrew *ra'*, depicts evil actions and also the painful consequences of those actions. In the vocabulary of the Old Testament, both the one performing evil acts and the other suffering the consequences of those evil acts suffer. As demons are inherently evil, it seems that either side of the action—the perpetrator side or the victim side—provides access to evil spirits.

Victims of sexual abuse need to know the love of a God who suffers with them, to receive His forgiveness for any sinful responses and to extend His forgiveness to the perpetrator. Often the loving support of other believers and the help of a wise counselor is needed. Just as often a person will need deliverance from demons who took advantage of the abuse to enter and further oppress the sufferer.

Sins of the Fathers

Many in deliverance ministry rely on a verse in Exodus to support the idea that the sins of parents or grandparents may plant a curse that affects the lives of their offspring. That verse is Exodus 20:5, which states, "I, the LORD your God, am a jealous God, punishing the children for the sin of the fathers to the third and fourth generation of those who hate me."

This verse is interpreted to indicate that a curse rests on the offspring of the one who sins egregiously. That individual "hates" or decisively rejects the Lord, leading to sins that curse the family line. Many deliverance ministers seek to identify these ancestral sins, to encourage the victim to confess those sins on behalf of his or her ancestor, and to help the victim forgive the ancestor for the impact of these ancestral sins. Then, in the name of Jesus, the deliverance minister will break the curse.

If, for instance, the grandparents and parents were promiscuous, many deliverance ministers would see an individual's attraction to and subsequent addiction to pornography or some other sexual sin as being in the demonic grip of a curse caused by the ancestral sins. If several generations have lived in poverty and an individual seeking deliverance has money troubles, many deliverance ministers would look for the root in a "sins of the fathers" curse, and try to help by breaking the curse. In breaking the hold of the sins of the fathers, these deliverance ministers believe that the legal ground for a demonic presence is removed, and thus the demons can be easily exorcised and the individual freed from the curse.

Other deliverance ministers have a different interpretation of this verse. They teach that this does not refer to a particular iniquity in the family line; rather, they say, it represents the accumulated sin of mankind, the propensity toward disobedience in every unrepentant heart. I find that the central idea expressed in this definition better depicts the sin nature, which all of us share as fallen human beings, rather than specific sins that our ancestors have committed.

The "sins of the fathers" doctrine in deliverance ministry requires careful scrutiny. Does Exodus 20:5 mean what either of these two groups of deliverance ministers believes it does? If not, how do we explain the way certain troubles often do seem characteristic of families over generations?

In Exodus 20 Moses is introducing the Ten Commandments, which will outline the basic moral principles intended to govern the relationships of God's people with Him and with one another. Like all of God's commands, the intent of the Ten Commandments is to bless by laying out options that will lead to a good and happy life and enable the believer to avoid choices that will bring harm or misery. These Commandments give us insight not only into the moral character of the Creator and Lawgiver but also into the nature of the principles that govern social reality. If we live by these moral laws, we will also live in harmony with God and with others. If we violate these moral laws, we will disrupt that harmony and bring interpersonal disaster. To steal or commit adultery, to covet or do violence causes a reaction that harms the perpetrator as well as the victims.

Among those who are most harmed by violations of moral laws are the children in the household of the violator. One example suffices. A child growing up in an alcoholic home where one or both parents are physically or verbally violent is significantly affected. Much research has identified just how detrimental such an environment is, and how the psychological damage done to a child is reflected well into adulthood. Whether or not this child becomes an alcoholic, as many do, the individual typically carries distorted patterns of relationship into his or her own marriage and childrearing. The sins of the fathers have an impact on (are visited upon) the children and the children's children for generations.

Viewed in this way, Exodus 20 should be seen as a warning, not as the statement of a curse. God's Commandments are rooted in the relationships of human individuals in society; to violate them has a disastrous impact not just on the sinner but also on his or her loved ones.

The prophet Ezekiel ministered to Jewish captives in Babylon just before the destruction of Jerusalem and its Temple in 586 BC. Like Jeremiah he sent warnings to the homeland, urging the people to turn to God. And like Jeremiah his warnings were ignored. The people back in Judah shrugged their shoulders and said in effect that there was nothing they could do. They quoted a saying to Ezekiel, one that seems to reflect an application of Exodus 20:5 to their situation: "The fathers eat sour grapes, and the children's teeth are set on edge" (Ezekiel 18:2). That is, we are going to be invaded because of our father's sins. So this is out of our hands.

God responded by totally rejecting this view. In the coming invasion there would be no treatment of individuals based on what their fathers did: "The soul [person] who sins is the one who will die" (Ezekiel 18:4). The chapter continues with a series of examples: a righteous father and a sinning son; a sinning son and a righteous father; etc. Again and again the prophet emphasized that God deals with each person individually. The individual's own actions will determine survival in the coming invasion.

Ezekiel 18 serves as a corrective to misapplication of Exodus 20:5. Yes, when a parent sins there is an impact on children and even grandchildren. But that impact is not the result of a curse. The impact is a result of principles that God has built into the moral structure of human beings. Despite the deleterious impact of parental sins, God will deal with each individual as an individual. A parent's sins do not necessarily or automatically give Satan or his demons a legal right to oppress an individual, nor are a person's difficulties necessarily signs of demonic oppression.

189

It is certainly true that demons can be and often are involved in many family lines. But an explanation based on the common interpretation of Exodus 20:5 seems highly questionable.

Soul Ties

The concept of soul ties in deliverance ministry recognizes the fact that anyone can be greatly impacted by interaction with significant persons, interaction that creates strong emotional and spiritual ties. Such connections or soul ties can have a positive or a detrimental impact, depending on the nature of the connection. Soul tie connections are sometimes envisioned as rubber bands linking persons. Depending on the intensity of the connection, the soul ties will exert a weaker or stronger influence on a person's life.

Deliverance ministers make a distinction between godly and ungodly soul ties, generally defining godly soul ties as emotional or spiritual connections that are beneficial. Examples of godly soul ties are the connection established between a child and loving parent, between husband and wife, or between an individual and a mentor. In the case of godly soul ties, these emotional and spiritual connections are positive influences that can be used by the Holy Spirit to strengthen and mature the individual.

There are many types of ungodly soul ties—connections that are emotionally or spiritually harmful. Some parents, for instance, keep their children dependent emotionally and control their choices. In psychological terms such parents resist efforts of the child to individuate and use the child to meet their own needs. This creates codependency that is harmful to both parent and child.

Illicit sexual activity creates another ungodly soul tie. The apostle Paul indicates that even casual sex with a prostitute creates a significant "one flesh" connection (see 1 Corinthians 6:16). Promiscuous sex has various negative repercussions if the promiscuous person marries. Deliverance ministers are convinced that all intercourse creates a soul tie connection that must be dealt with. If married individuals daydream about their first loves, even when there was no sexual contact, they are considered to be linked by an ungodly soul tie. The "what if" or "if only" thinking negatively impacts the marriage. Another classic example of an ungodly soul tie is the connection established between a sexual predator and the victim. The abuse can have devastating and lifelong impact. Deliverance ministers also believe that individuals can have ungodly soul ties to groups or organizations, especially organizations that require members to swear oaths, such as Freemasonry.

Therapists and counselors are familiar with the dynamics of what those in deliverance ministry call soul ties, though the terminology differs. The first steps therapists and deliverance ministers take are similar. They help clients identify past experiences that created the soul tie and work to understand present problems in the light of those experiences. But while the therapist helps the client resolve the issues that the earlier experiences caused, the deliverance minister takes a more direct approach and seeks to break the tie.

Breaking soul ties is generally a matter of confessing or acknowledging any emotional or sexual sins, accepting God's forgiveness and thanking Him for it. A deliverance minister will then encourage the client to forgive himself and to renounce any self-punishment, self-hatred or shame the client has felt. The deliverance minister will encourage the client to forgive the person with whom the ungodly soul tie was established, and release that person from the ties that bound them to each other. The final step is for the client verbally to renounce and cancel any existing ungodly soul ties in the name of Jesus.

One question: Are soul ties better treated by a competent therapist or by a deliverance minister? God is certainly capable of bringing healing through either one. And even though they might use different terminology, the problems caused by soul ties remain the same. One disadvantage of the therapy approach is that a therapist may be unaware of the likelihood of demonic involvement in his or her patient's problems. Deliverance ministers are aware that Satan uses the experiences that create ungodly soul ties to introduce demons into a person's life. In deliverance ministry, after a person has identified and repudiated ungodly soul ties, acknowledged any personal sins involved, accepted forgiveness, forgiven him or herself and, if appropriate, a perpetrator, the deliverance minister will then in the name of Jesus command any demons present in the client to leave. The process has removed any legal ground that the soul tie has provided for demonic presence, and the demons generally leave without a struggle.

Spirit Guide

Spirit guides are cast as spirit beings who desire to offer guidance, comfort and advice. Some occult sites offer suggestions for securing a spirit guide, assuring readers that the "sole purpose" of spirit guides is to "help" and "guide" the living. That help ranges from the life altering to the mundane.

Should you change jobs? Ask your spirit guide.

Is the person you're dating (or married to!) your soul mate, or should you look for someone else? Ask your spirit guide.

Is the traffic heavy up ahead and should you take an alternate route? Ask your spirit guide.

There are plenty of people who testify that they received helpful advice from spirit guides. If, however, some disembodied spirit showed up at my house, I would not be quite so eager to take the words "I'm just here to help" at face value.

Yet thousands and even millions worldwide welcome spirit guides with proverbial open arms. And, according to one website, making the connection requires little more than desire, an open mind and a good deal of patience. I have no data on just how many Americans claim association with one or more spirit guides. But with the New Age movement, which has morphed into some 150 neopagan faiths (paths), with the growth of Wicca and with some sixty supernaturally based TV series, the idea that an ordinary person can have access to a spirit guide is becoming more and more popular. While ancient literature describes the powers held by a sorcerer's "spirit assistants," and while spiritists and mediums traditionally claim to have a special connection to beings from the "other side," popular belief in spirit guides has now commoditized the supernatural, offering supernatural guidance to the man or woman on the street.

Before we are carried away by enthusiasm for this otherworldly guidance, however, we are wise to ask a few questions. Who or what are these spirits supposed to be? What is the basis for believing in their existence? What is the basis for assuming they are benevolent? And even if some are benevolent, are there other beings out there who are hostile?

Let's begin here. Who or what are spirit guides? That question is a hard one to answer. In the ancient world, as in contemporary paganism, people believed in a spirit world populated by a variety of entities. There were gods and goddesses, spirits of the dead, heroes and harpies, the evil and the good. Spirit guides may be drawn from any of these categories, although the ancients tended to look at them as demons. Today the general consensus in the neopagan community is that spirit guides are disembodied spirits who were once human beings but have "passed over to the other side" (died). According to one website, these persons exist in this spiritual state so that they can be available to share with others what they themselves learned from life. Since, according to occultists, these spirits supposedly live on a "higher vibrational frequency," we cannot see, hear or sense their presence.

Spirit guides are quite different from the guardian angels we were told about as children and read about in the Bible. The angels of the Bible are pictured as having an impact on what happens in our world and have even appeared as human beings. Take a look at books on Amazon under the category of angels, and you get the impression that angels are still actively helping God's people in real, concrete ways.

So if we cannot see, hear or sense the presence of spirit guides, how do we contact them? The answer seems to be that a person simply focuses and mentally sends the message *I want to make contact with my spirit guide.* As to how they respond, the most common answer is that they put thoughts into our heads. Many people will tell you sincerely that they not only have one or more spirit guides, but that the spirit guides have helped them. If we believe in a spirit world that is parallel to our world, and I do, I am not prepared to challenge their testimonies. At the same time I am not ready to assume the "help" spirit guides offer is as benevolent as their supporters claim.

The fact is, proponents of spirit guides themselves warn that there are evil entities out there. They even suggest ways to protect oneself when seeking contact. One prayer (I guess you could call it that) asks the god or goddess of one's choice to surround the person praying with "your protective white light," and further requests that no harmful beings be allowed access to the seeker. Most of those who believe in spirits recognize that there are dark spirits out there, but they reassure us that if we intend to contact only benevolent spirits, the bad ones will not respond. This is a highly questionable assumption, as 2 Corinthians 11:14 tells us that "Satan himself masquerades as an angel of light."

What if a person has only positive experiences with spirit guides? Does that not prove that the spirits are benevolent? Hardly. What if these spirits really are con men from the other side? After all, someone who wants to suck you into a scheme that is in *his* best interests will surely make it seem that what he advises is in *your* best interests. The good con men will provide some real bene-fits—until the trap springs.

Most Christians today and throughout the ages believe in the spirit world. Our picture of that world is shaped by the Bible, which portrays the spirit world as a realm created by God and populated by two types of spirit beings, angels (who are loyal to the Creator) and demons (fallen angels, who rebelled with Satan before the creation of the material universe). Deuteronomy 18 and other passages in the Bible warn against attempting to contact beings in the spirit world, partly because believers are invited to come to God directly for guidance, and partly because the only contacts humans can make on the "other side" are with demons. Biblical demons surely are con men from the other side. They promise help, but all they really want is—you guessed it—you!

I do not want to discourage any interest one may have in the spirit world. This is a very real realm, and what happens there does have an impact on us and on our lives. A couple of generations ago people bought into the notion that science had proven that this material world is all the reality there is. People ignored the spiritual and spirituality. Today there is an increasing realization that there is more to reality than the material universe. People are searching for more meaning in their lives than a pseudo-scientific outlook can provide.

When it comes to the search for spiritual reality, there is one thing that has given meaning to the lives of billions of individuals for thousands of years—personal relationship with the God of the Bible through trust in Jesus Christ. Any attempt to gain a relationship with a spirit guide is an overt rejection of Jesus and the guidance God has promised us in His Word. If a person truly wants supernatural aid, that person needs to look to the God of Scripture, who loves us and gave His own Son to die on Calvary in payment for our sins.

Spiritism

Spiritism assumes that humans are essentially immortal spirits who temporarily inhabit physical bodies for a series of incarnations that are needed to attain moral and intellectual improvement. It also assumes that through mediums these spirits can be contacted and have a positive or negative influence on the physical world.

Spiritists believe that communication between the spiritual world and the material world happens all the time. While most people barely sense the spirits, there are mediums whose natural abilities to sense the spiritual are highly developed. They believe that mediums are able to communicate with spirits and interact with them. The Catholic Encyclopedia describes ways the spirits communicate that "express ideas or contain messages." These ways include table rapping, automatic writing, trance speaking and clairvoyance.

Needless to say, any practice associated with spiritism is forbidden in Scripture, labeled a "detestable practice" (see Deuteronomy 18:11–12).

Spiritual Warfare

The fact that a spiritual war is taking place is emphasized in Ephesians 6:11–12. There Paul warns believers:

> Put on the full armor of God so that you can take your stand against the devil's schemes. For our struggle is not against flesh and blood, but against the rulers, against the authorities, against the powers of this dark world and against the spiritual forces of evil in the heavenly realms.

This and other passages, which indicate that we are in an active struggle against Satan and his evil angels, make it clear that we Christians are involved in what truly is a war.

Some in deliverance ministry, speaking of spiritual warfare, include pressures on us from the world and the flesh as part of the conflict. While Scripture indicates that evil spirits might well be involved in our vulnerability to the world and the flesh, it is more likely that deliverance ministers will take the emphasis found in Ephesians 6 and see spiritual warfare primarily as a believer's conflict with Satan and evil spirits. God provides armor to protect us from Satan's schemes (influences), as described in Ephesians

6:11–18. (For a thorough discussion of this passage, see my book *The Full Armor of God.*)

Deliverance ministers also view spiritual warfare as direct conflict with the demons who are oppressing or have taken up residence in the personality of individuals. This phenomenon, *demonization*, calls for direct confrontation with the demon or demons involved. This type of confrontation, as modeled by Jesus in the gospels, involves identifying any demons involved, undermining any legal right they have to be present in the person's life, and exercising the authority given to believers by Jesus to cast out the demons in His name.

Strongholds (Ungodly Beliefs)

The concept of strongholds is introduced in 2 Corinthians 10:4, which states, "The weapons we fight with are not the weapons of the world. On the contrary, they have divine power to demolish strongholds" or strongly fortified positions. This passage defines the strongholds that we have authority to demolish. Verse 5 teaches that "we demolish arguments and every pretension that sets itself up against the knowledge of God, and we take captive every thought to make it obedient to Christ."

Based on this passage, deliverance ministers generally consider strongholds to be entrenched beliefs that are rooted in satanic lies and deceptions. Some deliverance ministers use the phrase *ungodly beliefs* when referring to strongholds. There are two basic types of strongholds emphasized by deliverance ministers. The first type involves distorted ideas and beliefs about God. Some people, for example, feel excessive guilt and cannot bring themselves to accept the truth that God forgives them fully for their sins through faith in Christ. They picture God as hostile and punishing, rather than as a Person who understands them, loves them unconditionally and has sacrificed His Son that they might experience forgiveness and be brought into His family as His sons and daughters.

The second category of strongholds emphasized by deliverance ministers involves distorted ideas and beliefs about oneself. A significant percentage of individuals who grow up with criticism, for instance, have a distorted self-image. They have trouble viewing any accomplishment as meaningful and fear any kind of risk. This type of stronghold, like the first, is very destructive.

While distorted beliefs about God and ourselves can be planted by ideas common in the culture or by the words and attitudes of others, deliverance ministers are convinced that Satan's demons not only seek to implant lies about God and ourselves but also work to strengthen these beliefs. As the beliefs are more and more deeply rooted in our personalities, they become fortified positions from which evil spirits can corrupt our experiences and also serve as a base from which to launch additional attacks.

Paul's solution is to bring every thought "captive" to Christ. The passage makes it clear that we cannot argue a person out of his or her beliefs. But these beliefs can be demolished and replaced with truth. This is not done by any human agency or gift but rather by God the Holy Spirit as the captive individual is taught the truth of God's Word.

Deliverance ministers who deal with strongholds will typically try to identify the ungodly or distorted beliefs the individual holds, and then in the early part of the process of deliverance they will help the individual see what the Bible actually teaches. As the Word of God is taught, deliverance ministers rely on the Holy Spirit to replace error with truth and prepare the way for the deliverance process.

See *Demonic Stronghold*.

Trance Mediumship

See *Channeling*.

White Magick

See *Magick*.

Larry Richards holds a B.A. in philosophy from the University of Michigan, a Th.M. in Christian education from Dallas Theological Seminary and a Ph.D. in religious education and social psychology from Garrett Biblical Seminary and Northwestern University jointly. He has taught in the Wheaton College Graduate School, served as a minister of Christian education and written more than two hundred books, including theological works, commentaries and several specialty and study Bibles. Larry is currently a full-time author and speaker. He and his wife, Sue, live in Raleigh, North Carolina.

More from Larry Richards

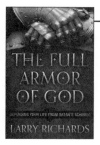

Stand firm against the devil's schemes with this ironclad, hands-on defense plan straight from the Bible. Using Paul's letter to the Ephesians as his guide, Richards reveals how God provides protection from every attack of the enemy—and how you can put on the full armor of God today.

The Full Armor of God

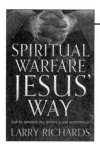

In this practical handbook, Richards offers a balanced, biblical approach to spiritual warfare using Jesus as a model. Drawing directly from Jesus' words and actions in the gospels, he explains how to recognize Satan's tactics, prepare to face the enemy and help others who are under attack.

Spiritual Warfare Jesus' Way

Exposing Satan's origin, strategies and destiny through Scripture, Richards reveals practical tools you can use to hinder the devil's schemes. Discover how to shake off fear, go on the offensive and win in the daily battles against evil.

Satan Exposed

✓Chosen